PARANORMAL
DORSET

ROGER GUTTRIDGE

AMBERLEY

First published 2009

Amberley Publishing
Cirencester Road, Chalford,
Stroud, Gloucestershire, GL6 8PE

www.amberley-books.com

British Library Cataloguing in Publication Data.
A catalogue record for this book is available from the British Library.

ISBN 978 1 84868 394 5

Typesetting and origination by Amberley Publishing
Printed in Great Britain

CONTENTS

ACKNOWLEDGEMENTS

The author gratefully acknowledges the following for their co-operation in the preparation of this book:

Sir Mervyn Medlycott, Anthony Gibbings, John and Kathy Chappell, Leslie Moul, Rosemary Cutler, Suzie Baverstock, Barry and Margaret Thomas, Mike Allen, David Haith, Angie Costello, Angela Thompson Smith, Alan Waters, Elsie Sanderson, Kingsley and Kathy Parry, Rupert Willoughby, Tara Hamilton, Geoffrey Lindley, Deidre Tucker, Stephen Tucker, John Liddy, Lavinia Barber, Matthew Anderson, Ronald Farquharson, the late Peter Farquharson, Douglas and Marie Williams, Robin and Mary Drake, Linda Flower, Dave Till, Matthew Anderson, Lee Perkins, Peter Knight (www.stoneseeker.net), Alison Crocker (www.alisoncrocker.co.uk), Scott Harrison (*Daily Echo* library, Bournemouth), Edna (*Dorset Echo* library), the staff of the Bournemouth Central Reference Library, the Dorset History Centre at Dorchester and Poole Local History Centre.

Photographic credits: pictures of Chantmarle House and 37 Abbot Road today by the author. All other photographs by Sylvie Guttridge except where stated in the captions.

INTRODUCTION

I have lost count of the number of people who, meeting me for the first time, have commented, 'Oh, you're the chap who writes books on Dorset ghosts and stuff'. It's certainly true that I have written books on 'Dorset stuff' – smugglers, murderers, mysteries, landscapes and villages, to name but a few topics, but one thing I have never written is a book specifically about Dorset ghosts. *Ten Dorset Mysteries*, published in 1989, did include a handful of ghostly tales but the majority of its mysteries were of the down-to-earth kind, so it can hardly be described as a ghost book.

In a way, *Paranormal Dorset* began life as an attempt to rectify this omission. 'If everyone assumes I have written a book on Dorset ghosts, perhaps it's time I really did,' I reasoned. What I did not want to do, however, was produce 'just another' county ghost book. For this reason, among others, I have broadened the scope of this volume to embrace examples of other phenomena besides ghosts and poltergeists, such as UFOs, doppelgangers, visions, remote viewing, out-of-body experiences and even fairies or nature spirits. Where appropriate, I have tried to dig beneath the surface of stories in an attempt to discover more than was previously known. In the case of the Lavender Lady of Corfe Lodge, for example, I have interviewed first-hand witnesses to update and shed new light on a story that has been told in more limited form by several other authors since it first appeared in print in the 1950s.

While this and some other stories (such as Sandford Orcas Manor and the Durweston Poltergiest) will be familiar to avid readers of Dorset books, many other tales will be unfamiliar and for most of these I have been able to draw on my 'day job' as a journalist in the county for the last forty years and the memories of one or two colleagues. I am particularly grateful for the suggestions of my friend and colleague David Haith, who wrote numerous stories on unusual phenomena during his many years as a reporter with the *Times-Herald* (later *Advertiser*) series in Bournemouth and Poole.

One thing this book does not pretend to be is definitive. Had the publisher's requirements on word count and delivery date allowed, it could have run to many more pages, and deciding which stories to omit was not an easy task. I am also aware that there are many more tales of paranormal Dorset that have yet to be told. With this in mind, the publisher and I are already considering the possibility of a second volume (or perhaps a revised version of this volume) and would welcome contact from readers who may have their own stories to tell or are able to add to known stories. Anyone with information is invited to email roger.guttridge@btinternet.com or write to the author c/o Amberley Books.

Roger Guttridge
August 2009

ABOUT THE AUTHOR

Roger Guttridge has spent most of his life in Dorset, having been brought up at Sturminster Newton and educated at Blandford Grammar School before moving to Wimborne in 1972 as the *Western Gazette*'s district reporter. He joined the *Bournemouth Evening Echo* in 1975, working successively as Wimborne reporter, chief reporter, deputy news editor and deputy production editor before becoming a freelance journalist and author in 1990. He is particularly well known for his historical series in the *Blackmore Vale* and *Stour and Avon* magazines and formerly the *Evening Echo*. *Paranormal Dorset* is his sixteenth book and his fifteenth on his home county.

CHAPTER ONE

ECHOES FROM HISTORY

THE OLDEST GHOST IN BRITAIN?

He has been called the oldest ghost in Britain, and those who saw him more than eighty years ago included a particularly credible witness. The respected archaeologist Dr R. C. C. Clay was returning by car from a dig at Pokesdown, Bournemouth, to his home at Fovant, near Shaftesbury, when he saw what he believed was a horseman on the chalk downs near Dorset's eastern border with Wiltshire. Dr Clay's location was 150yds past Squirrels Corner on the Cranborne to Sixpenny Handley road – an area that is particularly rich in barrows and other relics of prehistory. The horseman was on the downs to the north-east and travelling in the same direction.

'Thinking he was from the Training Stables at Nine Yews, I took very little notice of him at first,' said Dr Clay. 'Suddenly, he turned his horse's head and galloped as if to reach the road ahead before my car arrived there. I was so interested that I changed gear to slow my car's speed in order that we should meet and I should be able to find out why he had taken this sudden action.'

Before Dr Clay's car had drawn level, the horseman turned his horse's head again, to the north, and galloped parallel to the vehicle about 50yds from the road. The archaeologist continued:

> I could now see that he was no ordinary horseman, for he had bare legs and wore a long, loose coat. The horse had a long mane and a tail but I could see no bridle or stirrups. The rider's face was turned towards me but I could not see his features. He seemed to be threatening me with some implement, which he waved in his right hand above his head. I tried to identify the weapon – for I suddenly realised that he was a prehistoric man – but I failed. It seemed to be on a 2ft shaft. After travelling parallel to my car for about 100yds, the rider and horse suddenly vanished. I noted the spot and the next day found at the spot a low, round barrow.

A few years later, two girls from Sixpenny Handley made an official complaint to the village policeman about an incident that occurred as they were heading home from a dance at Cranborne. They claimed they had been 'followed and frightened' by a man on horseback. According to another archaeologist, L. V. Grinsell, writing in 1959, these were not the only incidents. 'Within the last thirty years, there have been reports, from shepherds and others, of apparitions having been seen in the vicinity of Bottlebush Down,' he wrote.

A Vision on the Cursus

It sounded like the last stop on a bus route or some deadly disease from the tropics, but author and speaker Peter Knight assured me that the 'Southern Terminal' was merely the official name for the feature marking one end of the Dorset Cursus. The occasion was a full moon on Friday 18 July 2008, and this rather impressive grassy bank in a field near the village of Gussage St Michael was the starting point for one of Peter's organised visits to ancient sites. Unfortunately there was enough cloud cover to thwart even the most luminous of heavenly bodies, but who needs moonshine when you have insightful beings to illuminate?

Peter Knight's insights tend towards the earthly but are spiced with the mystical. He's a man who understands more than most the power of earth energies, the forgotten purposes of standing stones, the significance of man-made lumps and bumps in the prehistoric landscape. There is an embarrassment of such riches in this part of East Dorset, including a holy trinity of mounds in this one small field alone. The Southern Terminal is one but just a few strides away are a couple of long barrows. All date from the early days of Stonehenge, which is just twenty-five miles away to the north-east. Looked at as a trio, not only do these three mounds line up precisely with the sunrise on the winter equinox but, due to their respective heights and positions on the gently sloping meadow, you could dash from one to another on 21 December and see the sun rise three times in a matter of minutes. Or you could organise three groups of people to witness three moments of sunrise

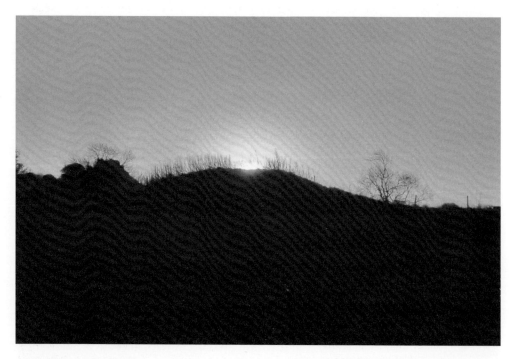

The winter solstice sunrise viewed from the Southern Terminal of the Dorset Cursus near Gussage St Michael. Photograph by Peter Knight.

from their respective mounds. It's an inspiring way to glimpse the cyclical nature of the universe.

The Dorset Cursus is the longest feature of its kind in the world, stretching 6 miles from the hill above Gussage St Michael to the Wiltshire border. In their heyday, Peter explained, the two parallel banks would have been shorn of vegetation to expose the full reflective whiteness of the chalk ramparts. How spectacular this must have been on a moonlit night. We can only guess at the precise nature of the processions and ceremonies that were enacted here by our Neolithic forebears.

Or perhaps we do not need to guess. Our earthly guide had barely concluded his inevitably speculative account of events over 5,000 years ago when one member of our party (known for her psychic insights) informed me that she had just tuned into those mysterious times. She whispered:

> I 'saw' a scene where a few young boys and men were making ready for a ritual. It was dark. The boys were covered from head to toe in a paste made from ground chalk and water. The ritual about to begin was to act out a second birth – the birth into manhood. These people knew that a baby is often reluctant to be born – it needs extra push (contractions). The womb is a safe place and some babies find the birth process traumatic. In order to encourage these young men to start their journey, a group of women (who were priestesses) ceremonially pushed them into the Cursus – one at a time. This was a journey that had to be made alone. Each young man had to walk, totally naked save for the chalk paste, along the length of the Cursus towards the light (a bonfire). Along its route there would be other women holding torches or tending small fires. They were to offer no help, just to show the way. The boys were primed to expect that they would be beset by doubts and scary things of the night, representing their inner fears. But when they made it to the end, through the birth canal to the light, they were considered born into manhood. For a split second I was in the mind of one of the participants. He was shivering, I don't think from the cold. He really didn't want to do this but he knew that he had to. He was determined to put on a brave face but he was thinking of his mummy and wanted to be with her.

The woman experiencing this vision in the twenty-first century made no claims for the authenticity of her insights, preferring people to judge for themselves. But she did express a strong feeling that the route was 'not as long as it seems today – perhaps half its present length'. Research on the Internet later revealed that the Cursus was indeed lengthened at some time during prehistory.

Whether this is a product of a psychic person's genuine insight or simply her imagination, we may never know. But there is no question that this was an important place to our ancestors of 5,000 years ago or that there are still powerful energies there. Even I, a self-confessed 'insensitive', had a dowsing rod turn powerfully in my hand each time I walked over a particular spot that Peter Knight had pointed out.

THE LAST ABBOT OF FORDE

Thomas Chard, the last of Forde Abbey's thirty-two abbots, was a monk who managed to keep his head while all around were losing theirs – in some cases literally. While his opposite number at Glastonbury refused to surrender his abbey to Thomas Cromwell's men during the dissolution of the monasteries in 1539, and was hanged for his stand, Abbot Chard opted for discretion. As a result, both he and a major part of his abbey survived, albeit with radically changed roles. Chard became Thorncombe's parish priest and Forde Abbey a private home, which it remains, although it is now also a popular tourist attraction.

Forde Abbey, standing on the Dorset bank of the River Axe, close to the borders with Devon (to which it once belonged) and Somerset, already had a long history when Abbot Chard took charge in 1521. It owes its existence to a niece of William the Conqueror who, in 1141, befriended a band of Cistercian monks as they trudged east following a failed attempt to found an abbey on barren land in west Devon. She offered them the Manor of Thorncombe and it was here that they built an abbey, which was to prosper for 400 years. Showered with gifts and bequests of land and money in exchange for prayers to be said for the donors' souls, Forde Abbey grew so rapidly that within 160 years it owned 30,000 acres in the three counties which surrounded it. Thomas Chard was a wise and dynamic abbot who presided over a major reconstruction programme and left Forde Abbey in a much better state than he found it. Despite his relative success in saving the complex from complete destruction, he must have been greatly saddened by the events which followed Henry VIII's fall-out with the Catholic church. Perhaps this explains Abbot Chard's lingering attachment to Forde, where he is said occasionally to appear seated at the table in the monks' refectory. Another account describes a figure, clothed in a monk's shawl, tied at the waist, moving slowly along the surviving part of the

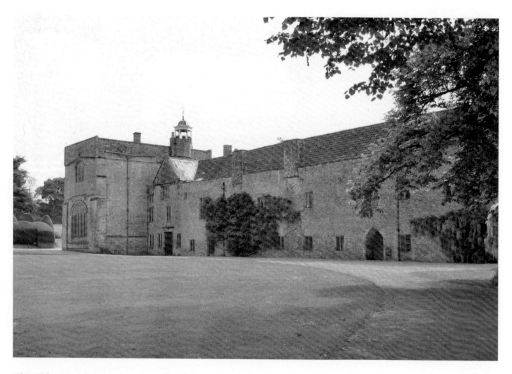

The oldest surviving part of Forde Abbey, dating from the twelfth century.

cloisters, where the monks performed their meditative walks. The cloisters once formed a quadrangle around the Abbey Church and the one remaining side is a relic of the renovation begun by Abbot Chard in 1520 but never completed.

Following the termination of its monastic activities, Forde Abbey was allowed to deteriorate until the next great period of national disruption. In 1649, in the later stages of the Civil War, it had the good fortune to be acquired by Oliver Cromwell's Attorney General, Edmund Prideaux, who had the will and resources to restore it to a level beyond even its previous grandeur.

A later Edmund Prideaux, the last of the Forde Prideaux, is involved in another of the house's famous ghost stories. Like many other occupants, his mortal remains were buried in a vault beneath the chapel. There are in fact two vaults, one higher than the other. The older, lower vault became severely waterlogged due to seepage from the River Axe, forcing one past owner to have the coffins raised above the water level. In 1974, in their book *Ghosts of Dorset, Devon and Somerset*, Rodney Legg, Mary Collier and Tom Perrott told how, many years later, terrified workmen fled from the chapel after hearing voices. 'Some took to their heels, declaring that the voices were coming up from the vaults beneath,' they wrote. In particular they heard two men quarrelling violently and 'strange thudding noises'. The braver workmen stayed to listen and concluded that both vaults were completely flooded, causing the coffins to float about, and that whenever Edmund Prideaux's coffin collided with that of Francis Gwyn (husband of Edmund's daughter and heir, Margaret), they noisily resumed their quarrel.

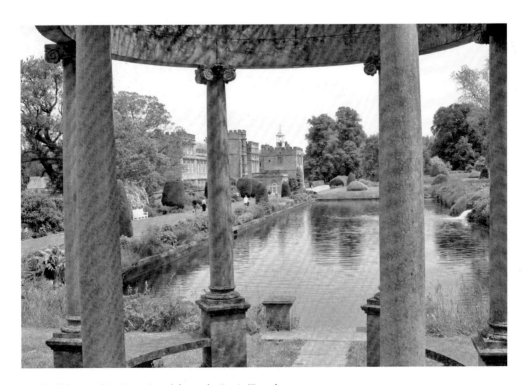

Forde Abbey and its Long Pond from the Ionic Temple.

Legg and friends doubted that the vaults had ever been completely awash or that lead coffins weighing six hundredweights each would have floated. They put forward an alternative theory that the voices and other noises were due to 'some trick of acoustics'. In 1978, however, this in turn was challenged by Mrs Mark Roper, whose husband's family succeeded the Gwyns at Forde. She told *Pulman's Weekly News* reporter Chris Carson that the vaults definitely had been awash and were filled with earth because of the eerie noises. Carson reported that the vaults were again flooded at the time of his visit but that although the water was waist-deep, 'the coffins seemed well-secured'. But he added, 'Ghosts or not, Mrs Roper said she would not care to go down there alone'.

PURBECK'S PHANTOM ARMY

England was a nation at its most sensitive in 1678, the result of a new wave of anti-Catholic persecution and an event known to history students as the Popish Plot. This was a story cooked up by Dr Israel Tonge and a sacked Anglican clergyman called Titus Oates who, on oath to a London magistrate, revealed details of an alleged plot to assassinate Charles II, murder thousands of Protestants and install his brother, James, Duke of York, a Roman Catholic, on the throne. There was no truth in the tale but the subsequent death of the magistrate by his own sword sparked panic and led to the execution of three innocent men for his murder, the dismissal and/or arrest of many eminent Catholics and the hasty departure of the Duke of York to foreign shores.

It was against this backcloth that, in the closing weeks of 1678, more than 100 people witnessed a strange phenomenon on the line of Purbeck Hills to the east of the cliff-top hill fort called Flower's Barrow. 'One evening in December,' Dorset historian the Revd John Hutchins reported a century later, 'was imagined to be seen a vast number of armed men, several thousands, marching from Flowers Barrow over Grange Hill; and a great noise and clashing of arms was supposed to have been heard. Nothing appeared over the south side of the hill.'

The witnesses included the respected owner of nearby Creech Grange, Captain John Lawrence, his brother, four clay-cutters, who were just finishing work for the day, and 'all the people in the cottages and hamlets thereabout, who left their supper and houses, and came to Wareham, and alarmed the town'.

News that there was an invading army barely 4 miles to the south was greeted with understandable alarm by the people of Wareham, who immediately barricaded the bridge over the River Frome and drew all their boats to the north bank. As 300 militiamen marched to Wareham to begin the defence of the realm, Captain Lawrence and his brother headed for London, where they repeated their story on oath to the Privy Council.

Whatever they saw on that day in early December 1678, it was not a real-life invading army, and we can only imagine the extent of their embarrassment when this became apparent. As Hutchins comments, if Captain Lawrence and his family had not been 'of known affection to the government, he would have been severely punished, the nation being in a ferment about Oates's plot'.

Although Hutchins heard the story from an older resident of Wareham, it is confirmed in documents, including a letter dated 14 December 1678, thanking two militia officers for their efforts in 'putting themselves in a posture of defence', and suggesting that the 'contrivers and spreaders of this false news' had been sent for 'to be dealt with according to their desserts'. A pamphlet published in 1679 described the event contemptuously as 'the Purbeck apparition' yet also used it as an argument in favour of a militia, stating that 40,000 armed volunteers had assembled in two or three days ready to take on the French had the army been real.

John Hutchins could not resist a little contempt of his own, stating that 'This phenomenon seems to have been owing to the thick fogs and mists that often hang on the hills in Purbeck, and form grotesque appearances of large craggy rocks and ruins of buildings. At this time the evening sun might glance on these, which, assisted and improved by a strong imagination, caused the spectators to fancy what never existed.' He added that similar phenomena had been seen in Leicestershire in 1707 and on Souterfield Mountain in Cumberland on midsummer day in 1735, 1737 and 1745, when 'a great noise in the north' was also heard.

Hutchins' dismissal of Purbeck's phantom army as the imaginings of gullible country folk was an easy option for a clergyman writing 100 years after the event. He does not seem to have considered that his own interpretation might be equally far-fetched, given that most of the 100-plus witnesses had spent their whole lives in the neighbourhood of Creech Grange. It is hard to believe that these natives, who made their livings from fishing, farming and digging clay, were so completely fooled by a local weather phenomenon that they sparked a national security alert. The Titus Oates affair rendered those in power in London a little nervous but it cannot have been uppermost in the minds of rural Dorset folk.

According to Rodney Legg, the ghostly army has a pedigree that goes back more than 1,500 years before the time of Captain Lawrence and his friends. 'It is said,' writes Legg in *Mysterious Dorset*, 'to be of Roman soldiers who leave the Worbarrow Bay clifftop fortress of Flower's Barrow and march along Bindon Hill above Lulworth Cove, especially when the current world is at war. People say it exists or that it is possible to uncomfortably feel an inexplicable presence. The thud of the trampling of horses and men is plainly heard and their indistinct forms seen as the fog drifts; "on these nights no rabbits and no dog can be induced to go near".'

Little is known of the military history of Flower's Barrow, an Iron Age hill fort that stands 550ft above sea level on the crumbling cliffs between Lulworth and Tyneham and on the edge of the modern British army's firing ranges. However, there is every chance it was the scene of a deadly battle after the Roman general Vespasian's Second Legion set up its base camp at Wimborne in AD 43 and systematically attacked the Wessex people in their hill forts.

GHOSTS OF THE MONMOUTH REBELLION

Two striking facts about the cottage ghost of Woodyates are the precise location (an old cottage on the east side of the Blandford to Salisbury road) and the date on which the apparition appeared (15 July in three consecutive years). The cottage was demolished many years ago, but it was still standing when Lt. Col. John Benett-Stanford visited Woodyates in the 1920s and heard a tale that intrigued him.

'Mad Jack', as the old Etonian was known, was a man of many talents, including career soldier (he fought in India, the Sudan, the Boer War and the First World War), early film-maker (his efforts included the only footage of the Battle of Omdurman in 1898), yachtsman, practical-joker, village squire, Colonel Blimp lookalike and seducer of virgins (he is said to have exercised his rights of 'droit de seigneur' among the local girls). But it was in his role as a historian of the Monmouth Rebellion that the squire of Pythouse, Wiltshire, listened avidly to Mrs Kirby, who had formerly lived in the old cottage.

'The ghost was the figure of a tall, good-looking young man, well-dressed and in a wig, standing in the middle of the room with the light of a summer's night showing through the windows,' wrote Benett-Stanford in 1937. 'He stood there for some time and gradually melted away, and on each occasion Mrs Kirby was disturbed by banging doors. Lighting a candle, she went out into the passage and found all the bedroom doors open, and as the banging continued below stairs, she went down and found all the indoor doors ajar and swinging. The Kirbys left after the third year and I believe the house has been empty since.'

What particularly interested the old colonel was, firstly, that the thatched cottage close to Dorset's border with Wiltshire had once been an inn where the fleeing Duke of Monmouth received a change of clothes and his last meal as a free man on 6 July, 1685 and, secondly, that 15 July was the date of his public beheading on Tower Hill.

Dorset is inextricably bound up with the dramatic events which followed the death of Charles II as Monmouth, his illegitmate son, attempted to seize the throne from his Catholic uncle, James II. Perhaps inevitably, there is an ample supply of ghost stories to accompany each phase of the extended story.

Near Lyme Regis, where Monmouth landed at dusk on 11 June 1685, witnesses claim to have seen and/or heard the ghost of the ill-fated Duke on his white horse late at night between Uplyme and Yawl. According to Rodney Legg and Mary Collier, one local family found the sound of hooves so convincing that they thought their ponies must have escaped and went out to look for them.

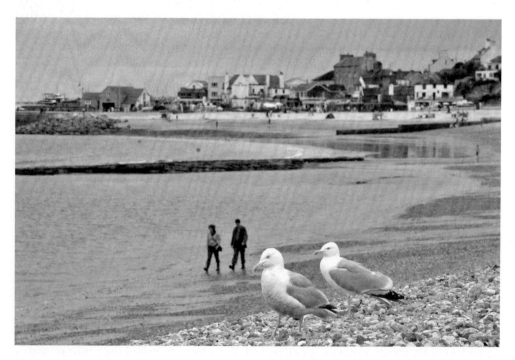

The shore at Lyme Regis, where the Duke of Monmouth began his attempt to seize the throne in 1685.

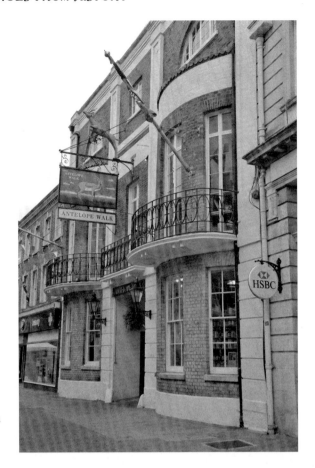

The frontage of the Antelope Hotel at Dorchester, where Judge Jeffreys conducted part of his 'Bloody Assize', is now the entrance to the Antelope Walk shopping precinct.

From Lyme Regis, Monmouth made his way north through Devon and Somerset towards Bristol, gathering an army as he went. After defeat in the Battle of Sedgemoor on 6 July, the duke and several companions fled back into Dorset, stopping at Woodyates for refreshments and to assume a disguise. From there Monmouth headed for Poole intending to sail to Holland, but he was spotted on Horton Heath and captured by an ash tree at a spot still known as the Monmouth Ash and taken to London to await his fate.

The episode had a grim sequel as Judge Jeffreys ruthlessly dispensed his 'justice' at his 'Bloody Assize'. At Dorchester alone, he dealt with 312 rebels in 5 days, of whom 74 were executed (in many cases hanged, drawn and quartered), 175 transported to the West Indies and 9 fined and/or whipped.

Jeffreys' Dorchester courtroom was in the Antelope Hotel, where he gave early notice of his intentions by having it hung with scarlet curtains.

Two hundred and seventy years later, in 1955, a guest at the Antelope, Miss Dorothy E. Warren, reported a series of strange events on four consecutive nights. On the first three nights Miss Warren, who took a keen interest in the supernatural, was woken by light streaming through an open bedroom door – although on each occasion she had carefully closed the door before going to bed. But when she raised the problem with a chambermaid, they could find nothing wrong with the door or the way in which she was closing it. On the fourth night the door opened again but Miss Warren also heard footsteps pacing back and forth in the next room and the occasional 'clink' of metal against metal. The time was 2.30 am and, as the footsteps continued, the exasperated guest called out, 'For goodness sake shut up!'

To her surprise, the noises stopped instantly, but when she made enquiries next morning, she discovered not only that the adjoining room was unoccupied but also that the wall was too thick to be penetrated by all but the loudest noises. Miss Warren – puzzled but still unsettled – was given a different room for the rest of her stay and slept undisturbed.

Judge Jeffreys' memorable form of justice left deep scars on the psyche of many West Country communities, not least Lyme Regis, where the Lord Chief Justice's visit on 11 September was followed next day by the execution of twelve local men at the very spot on the beach where Monmouth had landed three months earlier. At the Great House in Broad Street (later known as Chatham House), whose owner's support for James II and enthusiastic assistance for Judge Jeffreys made him a hated figure, the heads of two rebels were impaled on the spiked iron gates. Immediately after the death of the owner, whose name was Jones, a series of strange happenings were recorded at the Great House, including 'A mighty noise and a great light in the air, and the table of his house fell in, and the devil came to carry him away'. The story becomes even more bizarre. Soon after, the master of a British ship sailing near Sicily saw a 'strange craft looming in the sea-haze', hailed it in the traditional manner and was 'a little taken aback to find it manned with devils'. He must have been even more astonished when, according to the legend, the skipper of the satanic vessel replied, 'Out of Lyme, bound for Mount Etna with Jones!'

The ghost of Judge Jeffreys himself is also said to haunt the Great House, where he has been seen in his robes, a black cap on his wig and brandishing a bloody bone. By the 1960s, the building was in use as shops and offices, including the International Stores. 'Heavy footsteps at night have been experienced by the staff, who call the spirit Annie, while the older people of Lyme are more likely to blame the judge,' reported Rodney Legg in 1974. Among the witnesses was a store manager; according to the *International Stores Magazine*, he was alone in the shop when he heard footsteps moving across the room above. Knowing that the adjoining properties were also deserted, he made a thorough search but found nothing.

Another hotbed of Monmouth support was Beaminster, where the rebels included John Daniel, of Bridge House. After returning home from the Sedgemoor defeat, Daniel had a dream in which the archangel Michael urged him to 'go west'. He woke to the sound of the king's soldiers searching for rebels. As they arrived at his front door, he fled from the rear and headed for the family farm three miles west. Dashing into a barn, the quick-thinking rebel grabbed a hen and, still clutching his feathered friend, buried himself in the hay. When the pursuing soldiers arrived, he released the bird, whose sudden appearance convinced the soldiers that she rather than their intended quarry was responsible for the disturbed hay. He thus avoided detection.

Over the last 100 years or so, Bridge House has been repeatedly associated with hauntings, although for once the ghost does not seem to be directly linked to the Monmouth rebellion, except in that a well-known rebel once lived there. According to Amanda Allsop, who thoroughly documented Beaminster's ghost stories in the 1970s, the 'lady in blue' was first seen at the beginning of the twentieth century by Evelyn Leigh, a guest of the then owner of Bridge House, Mrs James. She described a tall, slim woman in a blue dress and high-heeled shoes, mistaking her for Mrs James herself and asking why she was walking around in such attire late at night. Mrs James denied all knowledge of the incident but subsequently began to see the lady in blue herself – so often, in fact, that she 'became quite accustomed to her companionship'.

Three or four decades after these incidents, a nurse arrived in Beaminster to look after the 1930s occupant of Bridge House, an elderly woman who had become seriously ill. Over the next few weeks first the nurse, then a temporary housekeeper and finally the owner's nephew stayed in the 'guest room'. The two women were both unsettled by strange experiences, including a mysterious knock on the door when there was no one there. When the young man was staying, the nurse was awoken by a succession of thuds, bangs, crashing sounds and groans. In the morning a tired and apologetic nephew was unable to explain why he had 'fallen out of bed without any bedclothes, and in doing so knocked over the bedside table and smashed the lamp'.

In a letter to Rodney Legg almost forty years later, the nurse, Mrs Vera Newbery, of Ludwell, Shaftesbury, recalled the following:

> Both the housekeeper and myself felt convinced that the guest room was haunted and one day, when we were discussing our experiences, the person who cleaned the polished silverware arrived. It was then we learnt about the ghost. She said her mother, before she was married, was in domestic service at Bridge House. All the staff knew that a murder had been committed in the bedroom over the dining room. This was the guest room. The blood had seeped down through to the ceiling by the side of the beam and no one could ever remove the stain. Of course, we all went into the dining room to see if we could find the stain and there it was – a dirty, cream-looking patch.

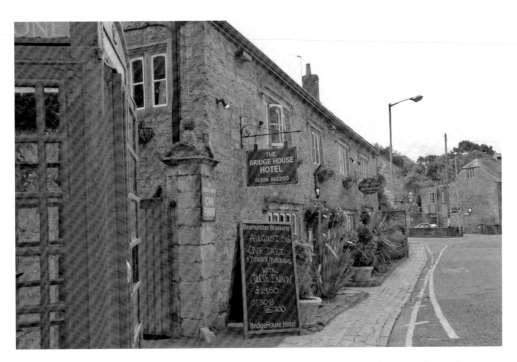

Bridge House at Beaminster, once the home of Monmouth rebel John Daniel, is now the Bridge House Hotel

The murder victim was said to have been a woman, but more than that has not been disclosed. There is, however, a further sequel dating from the time when the neighbouring house, Berith, was bought and demolished to facilitate an extension to the adjoining milk factory, contrary to the dying wishes of Berith's last private owner. Before the demolition, two local historians took about twenty photographs for posterity, two of which, when developed, were found to feature 'the distinct shape of a tall, slim woman in a long dress, wearing high-heeled shoes'. Both pictures were taken from the front lawn and there was no woman present at the time. Amanda Allsop claimed that the figure was a perfect match for the lady in blue at adjoining Bridge House. 'It would seem she had decided to transfer her haunt from one house to the other – and now she is homeless,' she suggested.

Bridge House, meanwhile, has survived to become the Bridge House Hotel.

THE WANDERING HAND

The story of a disembodied hand 'wandering' the Dorset countryside in search of its owner presumably owes more to superstition than reality. But the historical events behind this much-told tale are all too real. They date from a time when Cranborne Chase, which straddles Dorset's boundary with Wiltshire, was as much a battleground as an ancient royal hunting forest. It was a haven for smugglers, poachers and criminals of every kind and violent clashes were as vicious as they were common. Some involved poachers versus gamekeepers, and others saw smugglers doing battle with soldiers and revenue officials – often with tragic consequences. One 'very severe battle' between keepers and a gang of deer-stealers took place at Chettle Common in Bussey Stool Walk on the night of 16 December 1780. Local place names such as Bloody Shard Gate, Bloody Field and Bloodway Coppice testify to the violence of this encounter, in which the poachers were armed with deadly flail-like weapons called swindgels and the keepers with sticks and hooks known as hangers.

The deer-stealers were led by Sgt Blandford, a native of Pimperne and a soldier in the Dragoons, and it was he who struck the first blow, hitting a keeper so hard that his knee-cap was broken and he was rendered lame for the rest of his life. A second keeper sustained three broken ribs from a swindgel – injuries from which he died 'some time after'. The keepers struck back, inflicting such 'dreadful cuts and wounds' that the poachers were forced to surrender. Sgt Blandford suffered the worst injury, one hand being severed from his arm above the wrist. He was taken to The Lodge, where his wounds were treated and where a visitor noticed the severed hand lying 'in the window'. Blandford and several accomplices were later convicted and sentenced to transportation for seven years, but this was commuted to an indefinite jail term on account of their 'great suffering' from their wounds. Blandford was eventually released on an army pension, went to London and made use of his poaching background by becoming a game-dealer.

In a macabre twist, his severed hand had, meanwhile, been buried in Pimperne churchyard 'with the honours of war'. Blandford himself lived on in London and was presumably buried there, thus making permanent a separation which was considered wholly inadvisable according to the superstitions of the time. This, no doubt, is behind the story that the disembodied hand is often seen wandering Bussey Stool Walk in a never-ending search for its owner. Or perhaps someone really has seen the hand rising from its Pimperne grave or patrolling the lanes around Greenclose Farm and Bussey Stool Farm, north of Tarrant Gunville...

CHAPTER TWO

SCENES OF THE CRIME

MURDER IN THE HIGH STREET

Alice Green's maidservant Agnes Beard once confided to a friend, 'I pray to God I may live no longer than my mistress'. Her words were prompted by a conversation with a former mayor of Poole, John Beryman, in 1598 and they were to prove all too prophetic.

A few days later a passer-by heard the sound of barking dogs coming from the house in Poole High Street, where the recently widowed Mistress Green and her servant lived. A light was shining in the hallway but then the dogs fell silent and the light could be seen moving up the stairs to the bedrooms. All was now quiet and the passer-by resumed his journey.

The following morning there was no sign of life and a boy was sent through a small window to investigate. He was confronted with a shocking scene. In the entrance hall, lying in a pool of blood, was the body of Agnes Beard. She had been struck on the head and stabbed in the temples. In the main hall, also dead, was Alice Green. Her table was laid for supper and it was clear she had been attacked while eating her meal of buttered pastie. Nearby were the bodies of her two little dogs. Alice had been robbed of her inheritance.

'Murder! Murder!' cried the boy, and an investigation was launched. Several people fell under suspicion, not least John Beryman, who had recently expressed his dissatisfaction over the will of the late William Green, another former mayor of Poole, who also happened to be his father-in-law. Green had left the bulk of his £200 estate to his widow and Beryman had told Agnes Beard that he felt he should have had a larger share.

'You had your part already,' the shocked maidservant told him. 'I will have some before I am done,' Beryman replied. 'You shall have no more except you come by it by law!' exclaimed the loyal servant. It was a bold statement for someone of her social standing to make to a man who had already served two terms as Poole's first citizen.

Despite his comments to Agnes, Beryman's reputation suffered little permanent harm, and he not only survived the murder inquiry but went on to serve a third mayoral term in 1602. Instead it was one of his associates, Robert Hill, who paid the ultimate penalty, being hanged for the murders in 1599. Rumours persisted that Hill was not acting alone and in later years several other men came under suspicion. The inquiry was reopened in 1610 and again in 1638 but no other person appears to have been convicted.

Of Alice Green, nothing more has been heard, but more than four centuries after the double murder, the restless soul of Agnes Beard is said still to haunt historic Scaplen's Court in Poole High Street, where the two women are thought to have lived and died.

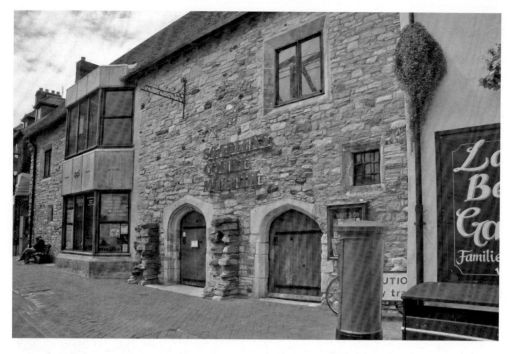

Scaplen's Court at Poole may have been the home of murdered Alice Green and her maidservant Agnes Beard.

Scaplen's Court is now a museum and education centre. Agnes is said to appear wearing an apron and to walk from the old buttery across the courtyard and up the stairs. Witnesses, including museum attendants, have also heard a dog barking even though there has been no dog in residence. In the 1980s Mrs Joan Patch told Peter Underwood, president of the Ghost Club, that the old town house had a 'warm and pleasant atmosphere' but added, 'I have often felt there is somebody there, although I have never seen Agnes – if the ghost girl is Agnes. But I have seen the ghost of a man with a white beard and wearing a cloak. Three times I have seen him standing in a room. He's rather lonely but not in the least frightening.'

FARMER BAKER'S HORSE AND CART

On a damp, foggy night in November 1865, a seven-year-old girl and her parents were walking along a road known as Murderers' Lane in the village of Melbury Bubb when they heard the faint sounds of something coming towards them. 'We heard the breathing of a horse, and then we saw it coming round the bend, pulling a cart,' the girl recalled more than eight decades later. 'The lantern lights were dim at first but presently we heard creaking wheels, the lights were brighter and the horse's breathing heavier. It was all so real and natural.'

The little girl's father ordered his wife and daughter to 'stand aside in the ditch and let Thomas Baker's horse and cart go past', adding that he had seen them before. The

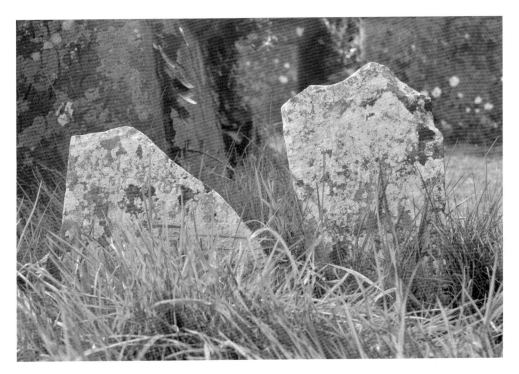

Farmer Baker's broken gravestone in the churchyard at Melbury Bubb.

father stood on one side of the lane, mother and daughter on the other. 'As the horse and cart came past, I shut my eyes,' the ninety year old told G. W. Greening, author of an article published in *The Dorset Year Book of 1949-50*. 'I felt so frightened, but I felt it pass; when I looked again 'twas gone. All around was the pitch-black night. But it's all so plain to me now at ninety as when I was a little maid of seven.'

A clue to the story behind the ghost of Thomas Baker can be found on a broken gravestone in Melbury Bubb churchyard. It records the death of the yeoman farmer Thomas, alias William Baker, who was 'barbarously murdered on Bubdowne Hill November 10, 1694'. Baker was driving his horse and cart home with two bags of golden guineas slung across his saddlebags, the proceeds of his sale of corn and cattle at Dorchester Market. Two men became aware of his riches and lay in wait on Bubb Down Hill. As Baker approached, one of them lobbed a stone, which hit the farmer in the head. Baker fell to the ground but his startled horse kept going and made its own way back to the farm with the two moneybags still draped over the saddlebags. A search party later found the missing man dead on the ground where he fell. But the robbers, by then, were long gone.

Seven years passed before any further information about the crime came to light – and it only did so then because of the astuteness of a publican, the landlord of the King's Arms in the nearby village of Evershot. One day in 1701 he was busy serving his home-brewed ale when he overheard two of his customers quarrelling over money – and discussing the killing of Farmer Baker. He sent for assistance and the two inebriated customers were overpowered and held in the Evershot village lock-up overnight. Next

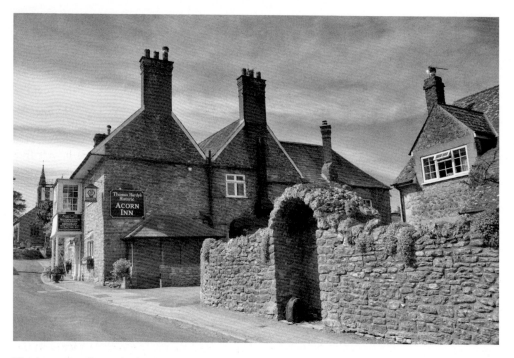

The Acorn Inn (formerly the King's Arms) at Evershot, where the landlord overheard a conversation between Farmer Baker's killers.

day, securely manacled, they were taken along the old highway known as Long Ash Lane (now part of the A37 Yeovil to Dorchester road) to the county jail. At the next Dorchester Assizes, the pair were convicted and sentenced to be 'taken to the tree by which they did commit wilful murder, there to be gibbeted in chains to suffer death. And we charge that none may succour them in their need and distress. And may the Lord have mercy on your souls.'

The task of making the cage fell to the village blacksmith at Evershot. It was made of iron bars and included rests for the men's necks and buttocks. The cage was fixed to a tree at the scene of the crime with the men secured by chains and guarded by watchmen to await their fate.

They were still alive when an old countrywoman named Martha Spigot, passing the gibbet on her way back from Yeovil and perhaps not knowing the order for them not to receive any succour, heard the killers' desperate pleas for water and took pity. She had no water to offer but instead fished a couple of tallow candles from her basket and pushed one into each man's mouth. Poor Martha also now found herself in trouble and, according to local tradition, was sentenced to seven years in the county jail.

The two murderers soon succumbed to the inevitable but more than 300 years later there are still reminders of their deed. The scene of their crime is still known as Gibbet Pit, while the route followed by Farmer Baker's horse and cart after his death is called Murderers' Lane. Meanwhile, the sixteenth-century coaching inn where the killers were arrested achieved a little fame of its own. The King's Arms became the Acorn Inn, and it was used by Thomas Hardy as the Sow and Acorn in his novel *Tess of the D'Urbervilles*.

THE GHOSTS OF JOHN AND HANNAH DANIEL

John Daniel's short life was overshadowed by tragedy from start to finish. The boy never knew his mother, Hannah, who died in October 1714, soon after he was born and just two years after her marriage to Isaac Daniel, a Beaminster smallholder. Isaac married his servant, Elizabeth Stodgell, in February 1717 and soon afterwards fathered a second son, Isaac junior. But in August 1726 tragedy struck again when Isaac senior became very sick and died. He was unable to write a will but conveyed his last wishes orally to the necessary three witnesses and a nuncupative will was drawn up after his death. In this he left five shillings to each of his sons and the rest of his goods and personal estate to his wife. He also exercised his right under the custom of the manor to nominate the 'Lord's next tenant'. He nominated John to inherit the tenancy of five acres of pasture and one acre of arable and Isaac junior to become tenant of eight acres of pasture and a half-acre of arable.

Sadly, John enjoyed his little inheritance for less than two years. In May 1728, some hours after he was sent out by his stepmother to tend her cows, he was found dead on a small island of sand and gravel formed by the current of a stream about 200yds from his home. According to one contemporary handwritten account, his body occupied a 'very odd posture' and there were 'several black spots round his neck and on his breast and belly, which tokens of violence'. The position of his body, the marks on it and the 'improbability of his voluntarily going to the place where he was found dead' combined to create 'great suspicion in the child's relations and neighbourhood that he had been murdered, which occasioned no small stir amongst the people'.

There was, however, no firm evidence, and Elizabeth Daniel allayed people's fears to some extent by insisting that her stepson had suffered from fits during his lifetime. Thus on 1 June 1728, John Daniel was laid to rest without even an inquest into the cause of his death. And that is where the matter would probably have ended were it not for the events which unfolded at the parish church three weeks later, on Saturday 22 June.

Exactly what did happen is recorded in two anonymous documents – the handwritten account and a letter published in the *Gentleman's Magazine* almost half a century later in 1774. The documents are generally consistent with each other but there are enough discrepancies to suggest that they emanated from different sources, which strengthens the case for the story's authenticity. Both report that Beaminster's schoolmaster, John Guppy, who taught in the gallery at St Mary's church, dismissed his pupils as usual between 11 a.m. and 12 noon

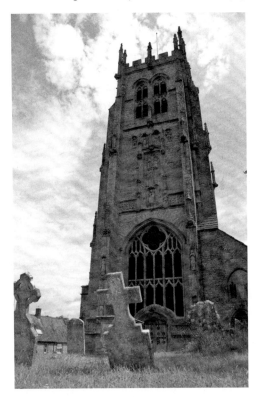

St Mary's church, Beaminster, where John Daniel's apparition was seen by his school friends in 1728.

on that Saturday and that a dozen or so boys lingered in the churchyard to play ball. After a short time, three or four of them returned to the church to clean up and heard a 'tingling noise', like the sound of a small bell or a brass pan being struck. The sound seemed to be getting closer and closer and they ran outside to tell their friends.

According to the report in the *Gentleman's Magazine*, the boys concluded there was someone in the church trying to frighten them, but when they went to investigate, they found nothing. 'As they were returning to their sport, on the stairs that led into the churchyard, they heard in the school a second noise, as of a man going in great boots. Terrified at that, they ran round the church, and when at the belfry or west door they heard a third noise, like a minister preaching, which was succeeded by another of a congregation singing psalms, both the last continued but a short time.'

The handwritten account makes no mention of the preaching minister or the singing congregation and reports that it was only one of the boys, aged about fourteen, who thought he heard someone coming after him in boots, which caused him to look back as he came down the stairs. 'At the farthest end of the school, he saw an apparition of a white coffin with brass nails lying on a writing desk there, at the sight of which the said boy cried out and leapt or fell down the stairs in which he bruised himself.'

The two sources are at one in reporting that the slightly injured boy was quickly joined by the others, four or five of whom stood in the doorway, from where they could see the writing desk. This group then 'saw the apparition of the above-mentioned John Daniel sitting at a writing desk, where he used to write when living'. He was in a writing posture and appeared to be wearing his school clothes and hat, which hung over his face. Because of the narrowness of the doorway, only the group of four or five saw the whole apparition, but all the boys were able to see the coffin with its brass nails and a piece of tape or gartering attached to one of its handles.

The first to recognise John was his ten-year-old half-brother, Isaac, who was reported to have remarked, 'There sits our John, with just such a coat on as I have, with a pen in his hand and a book before him and a coffin by him'. The boys resumed their game in the churchyard but returned to the church door from time to time and on each occasion saw the apparition again. Eventually Isaac Daniel, despite advice to the contrary, threw a stone at the figure, saying, 'There, Johnny, take it'. Immediately the apparition vanished, leaving the church in a 'thick darkness' for two or three minutes.

The story of the boys' supernatural encounter soon became the talk of Beaminster, fanning the flames of suspicion that had been simmering since John Daniel's mysterious death. Some of his relatives asked local magistrate Colonel Brodrepp, of Mapperton Manor, to investigate. He separately questioned eight of the boys, aged nine to twelve, and was impressed at the extent to which their stories tallied. One of the boys was regarded as especially reliable, being 'sober and sedate' and a newcomer to the school. Although he had never met John Daniel, he was able to give an 'exact description of the person of the deceased, and took notice of one thing in the apparition which escaped the others, viz a white cloth or rag which was bound round one of its hands. The woman who laid out the corpse for interment deposed, on oath, that she took such a white cloth from the hand, it being put on it a week or four days before his death, his hand being lame.'

Coroner George Filliter was sent for and immediately ordered the exhumation of the body. As it was being raised, two of the boys who had witnessed the apparition but had not attended John Daniel's funeral were heard to remark on the presence of the gartering on the coffin handle, just as they had seen it in the church. 'The sexton and all others that were present at the boy's burial did not remember that any such string or gartering was left in the handle of the coffin at the time it was laid in the grave,' says the handwritten account.

At 7 a.m. on 6 July, Mr Filliter belatedly opened an inquest at the King's Arms. The proceedings included the customary viewing of the body by the coroner and jury, which, in the middle of summer and following six weeks of interment, must have been a challenging experience. A surgeon also examined the corpse but was unable to say for certain whether there was any dislocation of the dead boy's neck. The jury were, however, told of the unusual posture of the body when it was found and of the black or blue spots found on the neck. Two women 'of good repute' testified that when they saw the body two days after death, they noticed a strip of black cloth around the neck. This was confirmed by the joiner who put the body in the coffin, 'for the shroud not being orderly put on the corpse, but cut in two pieces, one laid under and the other over it, gave an opportunity of observing it'. The jury were convinced and returned a verdict that John Daniel died of strangulation.

A jury's verdict is one thing but a murder charge is quite another. There was deemed to be insufficient evidence to enable the coroner or jury to point an official finger at anyone in particular, and yet there was no shortage of unofficial finger-pointing in Beaminster. The author of the handwritten document points out that John Daniel had been missing for a whole night before his body was found, yet his stepmother failed to instigate any search or inquiries as to his wellbeing or whereabouts. This contributed greatly to people's suspicions, as did a change in her deportment: before the boy's death, she was 'very gay, singing and merry' and 'has since affected to sing but it is observed by the neighbourhood that she pined away. Her lips wale, and in this time in an infirm way.' The document even implies that there may have been a motive for Elizabeth Daniel to kill her stepson, stating that not long before his death John, 'happening to be somewhat infirm, whither by the importunity or love or fear of his mother-in-law [stepmother], or what other motive prevailed on him is not known, but he nominated his said mother-in-law to be the Lord's next tenant to said estate after him'. The same document estimates the value of the estate at £300 – a significant sum in 1728.

Rumours may have been rife but there is no evidence to indicate that Elizabeth Daniel or any other suspect was ever charged or tried for the murder of young John. Again, the story might have ended here had it not been for two other strange events – one that happened a few weeks after the first, the other which occurred as recently as 1998.

Six weeks after the apparition of John Daniel, the congregation of 'devout parishioners' attending a weekly Wednesday morning service at St Mary's church included a fourteen-year-old girl 'of very good repute for veracity'. The teenager was kneeling behind her master in the gallery when suddenly she saw a woman push open the door adjoining the stairs and look up at the school area. The girl touched her master on the shoulder and told him there was a woman at the church door wishing to speak with him. The master, who had a sick child at home, feared that someone had come to tell him the child's condition had worsened and rushed down the stairs, only to see the door slam before him. He went outside but there was no one to be found. He searched 'behind the buttresses of the church wall and corners and all about but could see nobody, which increased his surprise for that it was impossible for any human creature to get out of the churchyard in so short a time'.

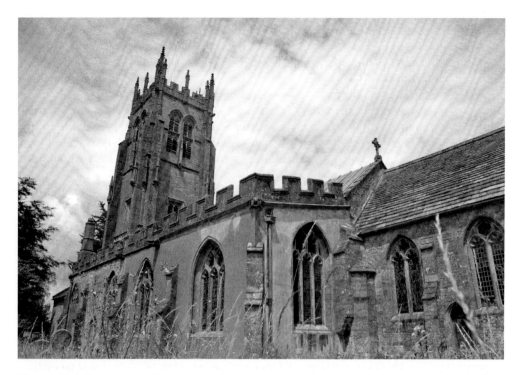

The churchyard was thoroughly searched after a second apparition was sighted six weeks after the first.

The noise of the door closing violently had been heard by the minister and the entire congregation and all were mystified, as there was no wind and no one in a position to open or close the door. The girl described the woman as being thin of stature, 'rosier with the pox' and with a pale countenance. She was wearing a 'sad' or dark-coloured gown, a flowered handkerchief around her neck and a straw hat. Those who heard this description said it amounted to a perfect account of Hannah Daniel's person and clothing at the time of her death in 1714. 'And it is to be observed,' notes the handwritten document, 'that the girl who saw her could not possibly describe her, being born about the time of her death.'

When I first wrote the story of John Daniel for my book *Ten Dorset Mysteries* in 1989, the sighting of Hannah Daniel's ghost in August 1728 really did appear to be the last word on this eighteenth-century mystery. I little imagined that the tale would have an equally dramatic sequel 270 years after the original events.

At 4.45 a.m. during an August night in 1998, Beaminster dairyman Peter Beer went into a field at Knowle Farm to check on some cows that were close to calving. He told the *Bridport News* later, 'One of the cows had calved and as I switched on my powerful torch to see where she was, I saw two figures standing by the cow just as if they were watching it calve. I picked it out to be a woman, because she was wearing a sort of long white gown, and the boy had a dark outfit. I was only standing about ten paces away. The woman turned around to look at me. She had pink eyes. The cow got up and walked out of their way. Then the two of them walked towards the graveyard and I heard the gates open and shut – that really spooked me.'

Mr Beer admitted that he 'half-ran' back to the farmhouse and was still shaking hours later. His wife said she had never seen him so frightened.

Could the 'spectral figures', as Mr Beer described them, have been ghostly representations of Hannah and John Daniel? There are reasons to think they may have been. For the field where Mr Beer's cows were that night in 1998 happens to adjoin the private, overgrown graveyard where many members of the Daniel family are buried; when Mr Beer returned to the scene a few hours later, among the graves he found was one of a man, woman and child – Isaac senior, Hannah and John, perhaps? 'For my own peace of mind, I had to go back and find out if there was a grave with a woman and child in it,' Mr Beer said.

He also described an event which, he believed, may have prompted Hannah and John to reappear 270 years after the original apparitions. Not long before, he was contacted by Daniel family descendant Rupert Willoughby, who wanted to see the family graveyard and approached Beaminster Town Council for help in restoring the crumbling stones. Could it be that this sudden revival of interest had triggered the apparitions?

Mr Willoughby, who has since become the owner of the burial-ground, is not convinced. He tells me:

> Peter Beer sounded very down to earth and I am sure the place can seem spooky at times. But whatever he may have seen or heard, I am confident it had nothing to do with John Daniel, the schoolboy strangled in 1728. Although he was the grandson of 'Sedgemoor' James Daniel [a veteran of the Battle of Sedgemoor and the founder of the burial-ground], there is no evidence that he was buried at Knowle – and the gates which Beer heard clanging did not exist in John's day.

Mr Willoughby, a Hampshire author, does offer one other ghostly snippet, however. In a leaflet he has written about the Daniels and their burial-ground, he refers to the burial of Sarah Anne Daniel at Knowle in 1773 despite her wishes to the contrary. 'The horses drawing the hearse are said to have shied as they were approaching the cemetery, as if confronted by her angry ghost!' Mr Willoughby writes.

Yet another ghostly sequel to the John Daniel story occurred in 2006, during restoration work on the parish church. A workman heard a bang on the south door and noticed a person's shadow through a crack under the door. 'He looked outside but nodody was there,' says *The Book of Beaminster*.

> Then a dark figure, whose presence could not be logically explained, was seen in the church. The following morning the trail of a child's footprints were discovered in sand that had been laid for paving and the word 'PEACE' written in the sand, yet nothing had been noticed the previous evening. Two days later the workman heard and felt a howling gale coming under the west door but when he looked outside it was flat calm.

THE GAMEKEEPER'S DAUGHTER

The Jacobean manor house, which formerly stood in its own park at Stalbridge, was once the fifth biggest in Dorset. Its most famous resident was Robert Boyle, known as the 'father of chemistry' and the man who gave us Boyle's Law, which instructs that the volume of a gas varies inversely to its pressure. Boyle spent many of his teenage years at Stalbridge House in the 1640s and performed some of his early scientific experiments there.

The house survived Boyle by less than 200 years, being demolished in 1822; some years before that, owner Lady Anglesey left it empty and in the charge only of an old housekeeper. One December she lent the house for the Christmas season to a friend and her children with the stipulation that they must do everything the housekeeper required of them. Among the housekeeper's stipulations was that the family must make a point of not being in the entrance hall at 5 o'clock on any afternoon. This was agreed and adhered to for some time, until one day when the visiting lady's family had some other children round to play. Their departure was slightly delayed and the lady found herself in the hall as the clock struck five.

'Hardly had the hour passed when her notice was attracted by a figure issuing from the door of one of the bedrooms on the first floor, which could be seen from the hall,' wrote the Revd W. S. Swayne in his *History and Antiquities of Stalbridge*, published in 1889. 'The figure was that of a woman enveloped in flames, who repeated to herself in an agonised voice, "I have done it. I have done it". The figure disappeared immediately into the door of another room.'

Lady Anglesey's friend ascended the stairs and was surprised to find that the doors to both the rooms from which the woman had emerged, and the one which she had entered, were locked. Intrigued, she decided to be in the hall at 5 p.m. on another day – and witnessed a repeat of the strange events. Mr Swayne says:

Now thoroughly convinced that it was something more than a mere freak of her imagination, she returned at once with her children to London, and took an early opportunity of calling upon the owner. She mentioned what she had seen and begged to know what was the meaning of it. The following story was then related to her. Some years before, the house was inhabited by a widowed mother and her only son, who was not yet of age. One day the boy came to see his mother and told her that he had fallen in love with the gamekeeper's daughter. The mother reproved him for his indiscretion and forbade him to mention the subject again. Not long after, the boy returned to the subject and announced his intention of marrying the girl. Once more his mother refused to listen to him.

Some weeks passed before the son broached the subject a third time. This time he told his mother it would be better for her to accept the inevitable, as the girl was already his wife and had been for several months. The mother was so indignant that she turned her son out of the house with orders never to return.

A few months later, however, the son was delighted to receive a visit from his mother, who appeared to have had a change of heart and indicated that she was now willing to receive both him and his wife at Stalbridge House. The couple duly arrived and the beautiful young wife did her best to please her mother-in-law. All appeared to be going well until one evening when the son arrived home from a long day's hunting to be met with the news that his young wife had burnt to death.

Mr Swayne continues:

The accident had occurred in this way. His wife had entered her mother-in-law's dressing-room about 5 o'clock in the evening, ready dressed for dinner. The mother-in-law was sitting in a distant part of the room before the looking glass and the girl stood before the fire.

28

Suddenly the elder lady heard a scream and, turning, saw her daughter-in-law enveloped in flames, having accidentally caught her dress on fire from the hearth.

The older woman's story was accepted without question – until the final day of her own life. Then, as she lay on her deathbed, she confessed to her son that she had in fact murdered his young wife by pushing her into the fire. From that day on, in what sounds like a classic case of karma, the spiritual law that we reap what we sow, Stalbridge House was haunted by the figure of the old woman enveloped in flames and proclaiming her crime. The haunting continued until 1822, when the house was demolished, the flaming ghost laid and, hopefully, the old woman's tortured soul was able to move on.

THE WOMAN IN WHITE

According to Mary Billington, a pioneer of women's journalism in Britain, there was, in Victorian times, a 'popular belief' that 'in bygone days' a murder was committed at a certain spot on the 'high road' from Wimborne to Cranborne.

In an article published in 1883, Miss Billington wrote:

The road passes through one of the woods on the St Giles estate. By the roadside are four or five magnificent fir trees, which give the spot a gloomy, shadowy appearance, making it in all respects a fit resort for ghosts. There is a form which haunts this place. They say it is that of a female figure dressed in white, and wearing a hood which covers her face. She paces to and fro, but as soon as one succeeds in coming near her, she makes a wild rush through the hedge. After this there is a crashing sound like a wagon and horses going fast through a wood, which continues for some minutes.

Miss Billington, the daughter of a rector of Chalbury, near Wimborne, implies a connection between the murder legend and the ghost story – presumably that the woman in white was the victim and that the perpetrator makes off at speed in his horse-drawn cart.

CHAPTER THREE

MANOR HOUSE MYSTERIES

THE SUICIDAL SQUIRE

Squire Light was in the blackest of moods when he came home from a day's hunting in January 1748, though the cause of his depression is lost to history. After a short time back at Baglake House, close to the border of Litton Cheney and Long Bredy, near Bridport, he went out again – but not before giving his groom some cause for concern. The groom, having a 'presentiment that something was wrong', followed him to a nearby pond but arrived in time to see only the final moments of the squire's suicide by drowning. William Light – thought to descended from the landed Lyte family of Lytes Cary in Somerset – was buried at Long Bredy on 17 January 1748, and the burial is recorded in the parish register.

Returning from the pond to Baglake House, which had been built for Light some years earlier, the distressed groom was 'accosted by the spirit of his drowned master, which unhorsed him'. The groom soon after fell violently ill and never recovered, 'one of the consequences of this illness being that his skin peeled entirely off'. He was by no means the only one affected by the strange energies that the tragedy seems to have unleashed.

'Shortly after Squire Light's suicide, his old house was troubled by noisy disturbances, which were at once associated with the evil deed of self-destruction,' wrote the journalist Mary Billington in the *Dorset County Chronicle* in 1883. She continued:

It was suggested that the spirit should be formally and duly 'laid' or exorcised. A number of the clergy went therefore for that purpose, and succeeded in inducing the ghost to confine itself to a chimney in the house for a certain number of years – it is not known exactly for how long. For many years after this, however, the place remained at peace; but on the expiration of the power of the charm, very much worse disturbances broke out again. Raps would be heard at the front door; steps in the passage and on the stairs; doors opening and closing. The rustle of ladies dressed in silk was audible in the drawing-room, and from that room the sound was traced into a summer-house in the garden. The crockery would all be violently moved, and at certain rare intervals a male figure, dressed in old-fashioned costume, is said to have made itself visible and walked about the house. The neighbours say these extraordinary occurrences continued for many years. They believe it most fervently, and are of opinion that as long as the house stands it will be thus troubled.

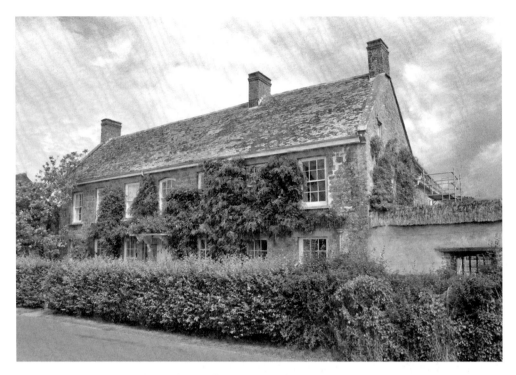

Baglake House at Litton Cheney, home of the suicidal village squire William Light.

Baglake is now the home of Lavinia and Robin Barber, who say it's more than fifty years since anyone saw the ghost. 'The son of the family we bought the house from saw it when he was a boy but he is probably about sixty now,' said Lavinia.

THE BONES OF WAT PERKINS

Who was Wat Perkins? It's a question that those who lived at Chantmarle House, near Cattistock, in the eighteenth century asked themselves repeatedly. The E-shaped building was reputed to have more than one ghostly inhabitant, including 'the Lady Ann', an apparition seen regularly in the late 1700s by servants as she passed through a particular room. The witnesses would often declare their intention to retire early or they would soon 'see the Lady Ann'.

Ann seems to have been a harmless ghost, but for some years in the eighteenth century there was an altogether more sinister occurrence. It happened in the hall at Chantmarle House at about the same date every year, when a shrill, piercing voice was heard to cry, 'Search for the bones of Wat Perkins'. The instruction was repeated three times.

The inhabitants found the voice quite alarming and feared that something dreadful must have befallen Mr Perkins at some time in the past, but they had never known anyone of that name nor had they any idea where to begin looking for his bones. Then, one day, fate lent a hand.

Some labourers working to remove a hedge near Kit Whistle, a cottage a little distance from Chantmarle, discovered a human skeleton – minus the skull. They

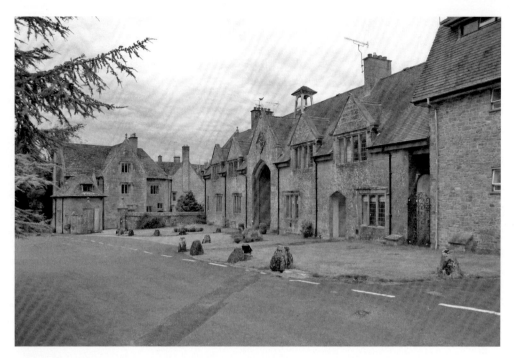

Chantmarle House, near Cattistock, where a shrill voice urged inhabitants to 'search for the bones of Wat Perkins'.

immediately took news of their find to Kit Whistle, whose occupant was a widow who supplemented her income by providing refreshments for passers-by. Clearly panic-stricken, the woman offered to give the workmen her 'best cow' if they would keep news of the discovery to themselves. Her desperate pleas were in vain, however, and before long she found herself being questioned about the skeleton. After a long interrogation, she eventually admitted that the dead man's skull could be found hidden under the 'yeath-stone' – meaning the hearth-stone. She then revealed that the bones belonged to a Scottish hawker who, some twenty-two years earlier, had arrived at her house with a pack of drapery. During his visit the unfortunate man fell asleep and, as he dozed with his head resting on the arm of a settle or high-backed bench, the widow murdered him by chopping his throat with a sharp hook. Her motive was to rob him of his drapery. To those who knew her, the woman's confession suddenly made sense of one of her favourite comments. Whenever anyone talked to her about their own clothing, she would counter with the strange boast that she had 'burned better things than those'.

The story was first made public in 1886 by H. Nobbs Cox in his *History of Cattistock*, published in the *Dorset County Chronicle*. He identified his source as a woman whose life spanned the years 1777 to 1849 and who, in turn, had heard the tale from people who personally remembered the events unfolding. Mr Nobbs Cox's informant, a long-term resident of Chantmarle House, added that the Scotsman's killer was tried, convicted and executed – and that the strange, piercing cry calling for a search for Wat Perkins' bones was never heard again.

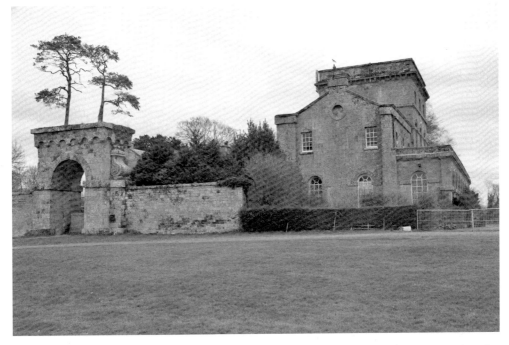

The surviving wing of eighteenth-century Eastbury House, Tarrant Gunville, which was once one of the grandest houses in England.

THE TARRANT VALLEY VAMPIRE

According to tradition, the ghost of William Doggett can be recognised by the yellow silk ribbons that tie in his breeches at the knee. The one-time steward of Eastbury House at Tarrant Gunville is said to appear headless as he drives around the park in a spectral coach-and-four, contemplating the lost grandeur of a house that was once one of the finest in England. There is also talk of Doggett being a vampire come back to haunt the village, where his body is supposed to have been dug up sixty years after his death and found not to have decomposed. In the surviving wing of Eastbury House, stories are told of doors that open by themselves and of the sounds of an invisible person moving about. Some have refused to sleep in the room where Doggett is reputed to have shot himself dead more than 200 years ago after cheating his employer out of thousands of pounds.

The best clues to the true-life events behind the Doggett legend can be found pasted into a book of vestry minutes at Tarrant Gunville church. The Revd William H. Hitchcock, who was rector from 1889 to 1900, refers in his notes to the appearance of Doggett's name in the parish burials register for 1786 and tells us 'a strange story is told of a suicide, and burial in the church porch, of a steward to Eastbury of this name and date! That in the constant absence of the then owner, Duke of Buckingham, he took upon himself to pull down large portions of Eastbury House and other houses were built of the materials. At last tidings of the same spoilation reached the Duke's ears, and on his coming to inspect for himself, the steward Doggett blew his brains out, the woodwork of the room bearing the marks of blood when restored to Mr Farquharson (from whom I had this history July 1899). WHH.'

Bryanston School, Tarrant Gunville Rectory and the Manor House at Ashmore are among the buildings that include stone from Doggett's misguided enterprise. But what of the other elements of the Doggett legend – the bloodstains on the floor at Eastbury House, the headless spectre riding madly around the park in a coach-and-four, the claims that the old steward's corpse had failed to decompose after sixty years in the grave?

The tale of the bloodstains is easily disposed of. The late Peter Farquharson, who was born at Eastbury in 1909, told me, in 1989, 'My father used to put a little red ink down by the fireplace in the Green Room, then tell people it was the blood of William Doggett, which had never gone'.

While no one claims to have seen the 'headless spectre' in the park recently, another of Eastbury's ghost stories is less easily dealt with. Peter said:

I haven't seen the ghost myself, but I admit that I'm a coward and it would terrify me. I would not sleep in the Green Room myself and I know others who would never stay there. I knew an actress who stayed there once and swore that she had seen a ghost. And during the war three nurses came down from Liverpool, arriving in the middle of the night. They were put in the room and at 4 or 4.30 in the morning they were out on the landing saying they couldn't sleep there. Then there was the little black spaniel I had with me as I was going to bed one night. He must have seen something that terrified him because he suddenly stopped on the stairs and just wouldn't move.

Of the claim that Doggett's corpse was found not to have decomposed after sixty years in his church porch grave there is, of course, no direct evidence. But there is circumstantial evidence that the old steward's body may have been exhumed around that time, as major rebuilding work in 1844-45 included 'lowering the ground from the porch round the tower to the north side'.

THE GHOST OF AUNT CHARLOTTE

The grand building that today houses Bryanston School, near Blandford, was built by the Portman family in the 1890s, but it was in their previous home a little nearer the River Stour that the ghost of Aunt Charlotte was seen. A maid who worked for the family in about 1870 told in later life about her first encounter with the apparition. It was her first night in the house and she was in bed when the bedroom door opened and a woman entered, stared at her for a time, then left. Next morning at breakfast, the frightened maid asked the Portmans' housekeeper who the lady was who had mistaken her room – only to be told there were no visitors. According to one version of the story, published in 1935, the housekeeper was showing her around the house when the maid suddenly pointed to a portrait and declared, 'That's the lady who came into my room last night'. The housekeeper replied, in a tone of surprise, 'Why, that's old Aunt Charlotte. She has been dead for years.'

A later version suggests that the housekeeper responded without surprise, claiming that Aunt Charlotte was seen so often that people ignored her and adding that she was completely harmless. The same account claims that it was not until many years later that the maid saw the Gainsborough portrait of 'Aunt Charlotte' hanging prominently above the stairs at nearby Knighton House, by then the home of Lord Seymour Portman.

Another Bryanston tradition is that an old nurse, attending the first Viscount Portman during his last illness, commented that she often heard walking and talking in his lordship's room at night. More than once she went into the room to investigate, only to find Lord Portman sound asleep. But when she mentioned it to his lordship, he told her, 'Oh, that often happens. It's nothing to hurt.'

When the old house was pulled down, an old woman is said to have quoted the adage that anyone 'taking the roof off a ghost' is condemning themselves to bad luck in the future. Some have dated the decline of the Portmans from this time, though it has to be said that for various reasons a great many landed families suffered a major decline in their fortunes in the early decades of the twentieth century.

SECRETS OF SANDFORD ORCAS

With reports of at least fourteen separate ghosts (some sources suggest as many as twenty-two), Sandford Orcas Manor, near Sherborne, has understandably been dubbed the 'most haunted house in Dorset' – or even 'in Britain'. Yet there are many who prefer to see it as the best case of 'apparition fraud' on record – including the present owner, Sir Mervyn Medlycott, whose family have lived there for more than 250 years.

Almost all the alleged sightings date from the period 1965 to 1978, when the sixteenth-century manor house was leased by Sir Christopher Medlycott to Colonel and Mrs Francis Claridge. From an early stage the Claridges claimed to have heard the sounds of 'beautiful music' from a spinet or harpsichord and of footsteps, voices and moving furniture. They described a number of ghostly figures, witnessed by themselves and others, including a lady in red, another in white, a young woman in black, a farmer in a white smock, a young man looking at a stained glass window, a screaming sea cadet, an Elizabethan walker, a fox terrier dog, a priest who tried to smother guests with his cloak and, most sinister of all, a tall, Georgian footman, who preyed on serving maids when alive and who, in ghostly form, smelt of decaying flesh and would not appear to any woman who was not a virgin. Colonel Claridge claimed to have witnesses and back-up stories galore, including one A. W. Daniell, who had lived there as a ten-year-old in about 1900. 'He came to see us in 1965 to say that a very nice old lady with a red shawl visited him on numerous occasions whilst sleeping in the solar room, which was his bedroom,' said the Colonel, 'and two young girls, now grown-up, informed us that when they slept in the solar years later, the same old lady used to visit them.'

Colonel Claridge claimed that the ghost in a smock was that of James Davidge, a tenant farmer alleged to have hanged himself in the arch of the gatehouse. The sea cadet was said to have been confined to his room for life after killing another cadet at Dartmouth Naval College. 'His screams of madness can still be heard today.' The 'white lady' had been seen on the stairs to the accompaniment of music, footsteps and 'loud knocks and weird dragging sounds'. There was a story that the ghost of the late Sir Hubert Medlycott was among those haunting his old abode. There were even claims that some of the ghostly forms had been captured on photographs.

The Claridges' claims attracted massive publicity, which in turn drew vast numbers of paying visitors to Sandford Orcas Manor. They welcomed the publicity, saying that they

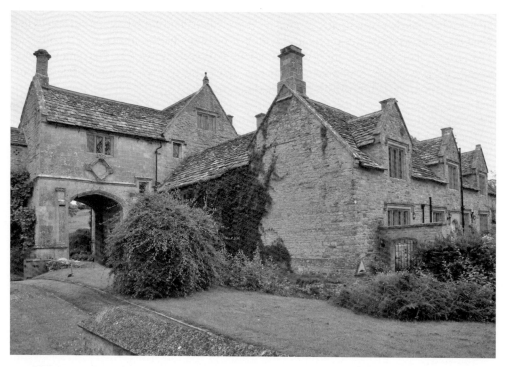

Sandford Orcas Manor's reputation may owe more to an enterprising tenant than any genuine hauntings.

were raising money to build a cancer research laboratory on the site. Support for the claims came from several quarters, including a team from the Paraphysical Laboratory, who spent a night there and declared there was a 'prima facie case for this house being haunted'.

In a letter to the *Evening Echo*, Miss M. Gallo, of Hinton Admiral, wrote that when her parents worked at Sandford Orcas, she and her sister heard knocking on doors, windows opening and closing and curtains being drawn back and forth. 'At the time our parents didn't believe us, as we were small – about six and five.'

Mrs J. N. Grange-Bennett, of Brudenell Avenue, Poole, who was born at Sandford Orcas Manor, said her mother had always insisted the house was haunted. 'At night,' she wrote in her own letter to the *Evening Echo*, 'bells would ring, upstairs windows would open and footsteps were often heard on the stone staircase leading to the bedrooms. My mother's small terrier, which slept at the foot of a four-poster bed, would become almost hysterical, growling and barking, apparently at some unseen presence.'

On the face of it, such stories sound convincing, as far as they go, and it may well be that there are elements of truth in the tales of hauntings – although the Medlycotts would not even go that far. Sandford Orcas's problem is that as its potential as a cash-cow became more evident, its ghosts became correspondingly numerous and the stories about them ever more fantastic. Recalling a coach trip to the house by Ghost Club members in 1975, president Peter Underwood noted, 'Colonel Claridge and his wife entertained the party with some fantastic stories: the huge gargoyles on each gable laughed in the moonlight; there was the sound of rattling chains every night; there was a room in which it was impossible to take a photograph; there was a phantom that appeared regularly seven nights running each year; a room that screamed; a room where "every night a man parades up and down, his footsteps heavy and clear…"; and so on and so on. Unfortunately the ghosts multiplied to such an extent that credulity was stretched beyond breaking-point; erroneous dates and "facts" were paraded; dubious photographs were exhibited; publicity was welcomed…'

Underwood was one of a growing army of sceptics, which also included Sir Christopher Medlycott. More than three decades later, his nephew, Sir Mervyn, who has lived there since 1980, is clearly tired of the whole business. He told me:

> People keep asking if they can hold all-night vigils here but the whole thing was made up. I think some apparitions are genuine and I wrote in my history of the village about the figure of a woman seen at the Mitre Inn. But the stories at the Manor started and finished with the Claridges and there have been further stories made up by journalists since to keep the ball rolling. Claridge needed to get more visitors to the house and this was a nice, cheap way of doing it.

Sir Mervyn added that Colonel Claridge, who died about twenty years ago, 'is six feet under in the churchyard and hasn't appeared himself yet'.

THE LAVENDER LADY AND CHILD

Lavender Lodge, a 300-year-old house on the edge of Corfe Mullen and Broadstone, was formerly called Corfe Lodge, and it takes its current name from the fields of lavender which covered 600 acres nearby. In the early decades of the twentieth century, the lavender was turned into perfume and other products in a little factory near Broadstone station. The lavender products were loaded onto trains for distribution across the UK.

Stories that the old farmhouse is haunted date back at least to Victorian times and first found their way into print in an article by Olive Knott in the *Dorset Year Book 1956-57*, reprinted in her book *Old Dorset* in 1958. 'The story goes,' she wrote, 'that many years ago a pretty young woman lost her child in the swamp not far from the Lodge and after that time haunted the premises and was seen hurrying across the heath towards the swamp. A pleasing apparition, she wore her hair in two long plaits and was dressed in a crinoline.'

The apparition has become known in modern times as the Lavender Lady, although her presence appears to predate the lavender farm. There has also been some confusion about the location with at least two authors muddling Lavender Lodge with the Court House, a triple-chimneyed Jacobean house which stands almost 2 miles away beside the A31 road on the other side of Corfe Mullen.

Olive Knott, who gave the correct location, heard the story from an elderly man called Billy Heckford, who lived in a hut on the edge of adjoining Upton Heath with his dog, Sparkle, five cats, two goats, twelve hens and a cockerel. Billy, who was about seventy-six in 1958, had worked on the lavender farm in his younger days and claimed to have seen the Lavender Lady many times. Once, he said, two of his friends, standing by his hut, thought they saw a woman approaching and opened the gate for her, but before reaching it, she vanished. On another occasion a group of men, arriving early one morning to work in the lavender fields, thought they saw a young woman, only for

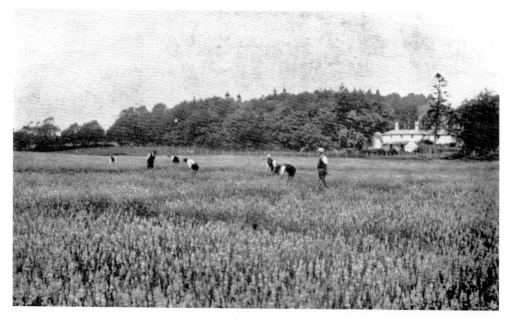

Lavender Lodge in the early twentieth century, when it was surrounded by 600 acres of lavender fields. Photograph courtesy of John and Kathy Chappell.

her to fade before their eyes. Billy also claimed to have seen a spectral coach and horses approaching Corfe Lodge and the figure of a man dressed like John Bull.

Billy claimed that his sister, who was a maid at Corfe Lodge, had also had 'many queer manifestations of the supernatural' there. This was confirmed in 1969, when her elderly daughter, Mary Cliff, wrote to the *Poole and Dorset Herald*. She wrote:

> My mother often told me about the ghostly lady at Corfe Lodge and I for one never doubted her word. She was a wonderful person, completely honest and sincere. She went to Corfe Lodge as a girl of 16. One night she was disturbed by footsteps and the opening of a door. Thinking it was her sister, who slept in the same room, she called: 'Is that you, Annie?' Then she became aware that someone was standing at the foot of the bed. Looking up, she saw this beautiful young woman, her hair in two long plaits, bending over the bed. The woman smiled and glided away. The next morning my mother wondered if she had dreamt all this but several nights later the woman came again. When this happened a third time, my mother became very frightened and refused to sleep in the room. She was then told that visitors to Corfe Lodge had seen the woman before but no one had told her this for fear of scaring her.

Mary Cliff described both her mother and her uncle, Billy Heckford, as 'too clear-minded and sincere to have imagined these things. The mystery remains and I often wonder if later inhabitants of Corfe Lodge witnessed any strange happenings,' she said. Mary probably died without an answer to that question but were she alive today she would be amazed at the extent to which the hauntings have continued and the number of correlations between her mother's experiences and those of more recent residents. At least three families have been aware of ghostly activities in the house and one of them is said to have moved out after a short time for that very reason.

Rosemary Cutler (née Dee), of Wimborne, often visited Lavender Lodge in the early 1970s, when she was friendly with a fellow student whose family lived there. She recalls, 'Once I heard the sound of a horse galloping across the back of the house and commented that it was a bit dangerous coming on to the road like that. But the family said it was just "the highwayman" and they had heard him three or four times before.'

Rosemary learnt that the family regularly heard footsteps in the hall only to find there was no one there. Objects appeared to move themselves, toys were played with by an invisible child or children and the door between the kitchen and a back-room sometimes locked itself. 'The family treated it matter-of-factly and didn't feel there was any threat. The family had six children and when the youngest turned sixteen it all stopped.'

John and Kathy Chappell, who bought Lavender Lodge in 1981, witnessed an astonishing number and variety of paranormal events during their eighteen years there, many of them consistent with the building's history. When they arrived with their children, Paul and Julie, then aged about four and three, the family were unaware of the house's spooky reputation. They soon discovered it for themselves. John and Kathy now live at Shapwick after leaving Lavender Lodge in 1999, and it was at their present home that they described the events to me in detail.

Like previous occupants, the Chappells often heard footsteps. To start with John and Kathy thought it was their children moving around when they were supposed to be in bed but when they went to investigate they invariably found that the youngsters were sound asleep. This happened not once or twice but dozens of times. Years later, research on the building's structural history revealed that the first floor bathroom, where these footsteps were often heard, had once been the site of an outside door with steps leading down to the garden.

Paul's bedroom was a focal point for much of the activity. Several times the young boy reported seeing a woman in a crinoline dress. In some of his sightings, the woman made hand and arm movements which suggested she was placing something in a cupboard. Once, he saw the figure pass right through the bedroom wall and several times he heard his name being called and even responded once or twice thinking it was his mother. Another time, while he was putting on his pyjamas at bedtime, a large number of books and ornaments suddenly fell from shelves above the mantelpiece for no obvious reason. Once, when Paul was asleep, Kathy saw what she describes as a 'white blob' above his bed.

Downstairs, the kitchen had three solid, heavy doors which had once graced Canford Manor a few miles away. One of the doors, leading to a utility room, had an old-fashioned bolt which was very stiff and difficult to pull across. Despite this, during one two-week spell the door somehow bolted itself several times. 'Most times it was just a nuisance but once Paul went through to fetch his bike from the garage and found the door bolted against him so that he couldn't get back into the kitchen,' says Kathy. 'He was only five or six and when we found him he was upset and crying.'

The family's two dogs were kept in a utility room and were not allowed into the main part of the house. But on one occasion they managed to find their way down the main staircase even though there were two closed doors blocking their path. Thirty minutes after they were returned to the utility room, they appeared again, tails wagging excitedly – and again both doors were found to be locked.

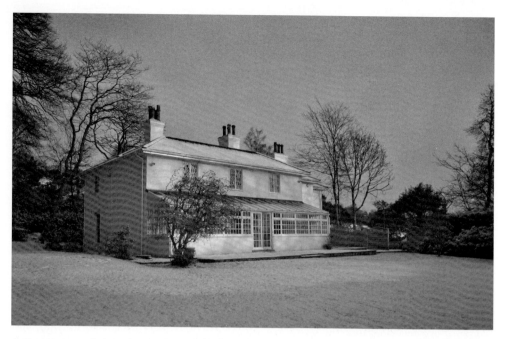

A picture-postcard view of Lavender Lodge during the winter of 2008-09. Photograph by Suzie Baverstock.

At least five or six visitors to Lavender Lodge reported feeling 'coldness' in certain parts of the building, including the cloakroom. Two babysitters reported seeing the ghostly figure of a woman despite having no prior knowledge of any hauntings. They described her as wearing a crinoline dress and having long, plaited hair but having no legs or feet. Like Paul, they saw her walk through a wall. Previous owners of the house admitted that they too had experienced a range of ghostly activities.

Many times the Chappells heard footsteps coming from the front door but they always stopped by the kitchen door, leading the family to think that the back door may originally have been located here. One day Kathy was about to leave to collect the children from school when she heard a child-like voice saying, 'Mummy, Mummy.' 'It sounded as if it was in the distance and I thought it was from the cellar,' she said. It was daylight then but when the same thing happened after dark in the winter, Kathy refused to return to the house unless her husband accompanied her.

Interference with electrical equipment was common. Lights repeatedly switched themselves on, prompting John to use Sellotape to prevent a light switch from moving. 'That stopped it for that moment but ten minutes later the light was on again and the switch had been physically moved,' he recalls.

Paul's toys included a Fisher-Price TV set and at 2 a.m. one night, when he was asleep, it suddenly switched itself on. His mother switched it off but an hour later it came on again. Another night Julie, then aged three or four, went to her parents' room to complain that her Fisher-Price telephone was ringing and keeping her awake. They advised her to switch it off, of course, but the youngster, hands defiantly on hips, replied, 'How can I, silly? It hasn't got a battery in it.' 'I turned it over to prove it did have a battery but to my surprise Julie was right – yet it was still working,' says Kathy.

One evening, when Julie was twelve, she and her mother heard a noise so loud that Kathy had to cover her ears. 'It sounded partly like a machine-gun and partly like a pressure-cooker that was about to explode,' Kathy says. 'We were both so scared that I asked her to dial the first two nines of an emergency call and wait while I investigated upstairs.' The call was never made, as the culprit was only an old treddle sewing machine which had been electrified. Somehow it had switched itself on and it now refused to be switched off except at the plug-point. When mother and daughter returned to the ground floor, they found that the television and video player had switched themselves on at 'an unnatural volume – louder than full volume'. Kathy and Julie took refuge outside, deliberately leaving the front door on the latch so they could get back in again – only for it to lock and bolt itself from the inside. They used a spare key to enter through the back door and were then met by a greatly amplified 'beeping noise'. The source of this was the children's Gameboy console, which had been missing for months but had somehow found its way on to a coffee table and switched itself on.

The happenings continued on and off for about twelve years, and Kathy remembers the last couple of events clearly. One evening in about 1993 she was alone in the house and painting the kitchen ceiling when she heard footsteps coming from the front door back to the kitchen door. She thought it must be her husband, who had gone to a committee meeting, and shouted, 'What have you forgotten?' There was no reply. She heard the footsteps twice more that evening along with the sound of the heavy door opening and slamming. The footsteps seemed to go to the cellar. When she heard the sounds a fourth time at 10.30 p.m., John Chappell walked through the door and Kathy was so shocked by his sudden appearance that she screamed and threw paint all over him!

Two days later, it was Julie's turn to be alone in the house after she came home from boarding school for the holidays. 'We had made a point of not telling her and Paul about the latest footsteps but I came home from shopping to find her clearly nervous,' said Kathy. 'She had been sitting in the kitchen doing some schoolwork and the same thing had happened to her, three or four times.'

With that, the paranormal activity ended and did not return during the family's last six years at Lavender Lodge. Bournemouth psychic Leslie Moul, who advised the Chappells on their ghostly problems, had once warned that the happenings would continue until the children reached puberty. In fact, they lasted a little longer. During those years, the Chappells did consider calling in an exorcist but instead 'learnt to live with it'. The children even gave the ghost a nickname – Fred. Kathy, however, is convinced they had not one but two entities – a woman (seen by several witnesses) and a child (because of the recurring child-like behaviour and interest in toys). This would certainly fit the tradition that a woman lost her child in the swamp.

Leslie Moul believes this was the case. 'They weren't harmful or malicious. The child was playing with the toys,' he says. 'A child ghost like that can't get enough energy going to move physical objects on its own. It needs a source of more dense or earthly energy to use. Their daughter, Julie, was the source of that energy. The child ghost could harvest all this surplus energy. I told them that when Julie became older and her energy levels decreased, her energy would cease to be of use [to the ghost].'

Leslie explains that a child's energy is one of several common catalysts that contribute to hauntings. Others include a high level of sexual tension or the presence of someone with drug or alcohol problems. 'The physical body has a more dense energy force than a ghost,' he says. 'A ghost's etheric energy is much more nebulous than any physical body.

The physical body gives the soul's energy greater density. So that's why they need a host person to feed off. It doesn't happen when a house is empty.'

Leslie believes the Lavender Lodge hauntings relate to an 'unfulfilled childhood'. 'When a childhood is cut short, often the tragedy makes the people that it happened to want to stay there. Because their ghostly bodies don't age, they don't have clocks and watches, there is no day or night, the mother and child can stay like that for 100 or 200 years or more. But eventually they get fed up with it and move on. They are not trapped souls but are trying to fulfil the childhood that was cut short.'

As well as talking to the family, Leslie also spent time alone in the house to communicate with the ghosts. 'The [ghost] mother said it was lovely for the children to play,' he says. 'Mothers like to see their children play. I said it was for a short while, don't cause any harm, it will be OK. I told the Chappell family there was nothing to fear, that it was just playfulness.'

He added:

Just as they appear like ghosts to us, so we appear like ghosts to them. They are nebulous to us; we are nebulous to them. Each dimension is superimposed on the other – hence they can walk about in our world, as it were. It's a bit like superimposing negatives. Most of the time nobody notices it. But occasionally, when there is an earthly catalyst, like somebody with a psychic ability or a drug or alcohol problem or a child with lots of energy, then these two dimensions almost merge.

The latest owners of Lavender Lodge report no paranormal activity in their first ten months in the property.

THE GHOST OF ENSBURY MANOR

When Kinson, previously an outlying district of Poole, became part of Bournemouth in 1931, the Victorian health resort's acquisitions included a manor house of great antiquity with a colourful past. In fact, ivy-clad Ensbury Manor immediately became the oldest house in the Borough of Bournemouth with title deeds, foundations and some other features dating back 700 years. It also boasted one of the finest Jacobean fireplaces in the country. But it was not to last. In the spring of 1936, demolition workers turned the rambling old building, at the corner of what are now Avebury Avenue and Austen Avenue, into a heap of rubble as they cleared the site for a modern housing development. As they did so, they uncovered evidence to support claims that the house had once been a favourite haunt of smugglers. When one of the workmen put his boot through the floor of a passageway, he found himself sinking into a 'curious bricked cavity that would have made a hiding place for contraband'. It was shaped 'not unlike a coffin' and big enough to hold 'a considerable number of the small brandy tubs which the smugglers carried'.

The demolition failed to confirm another tradition of the building's past, but stories that it was haunted persisted to the last. Announcing the imminent demolition in March 1936, the *Daily Echo* held up Ensbury Manor as the seaside town's only genuinely haunted house. 'All the native inhabitants of the district are familiar with the talk about the Manor ghost, but apparently there is little known with regard to its personality – if a ghost can have a personality,' said the paper. It continued:

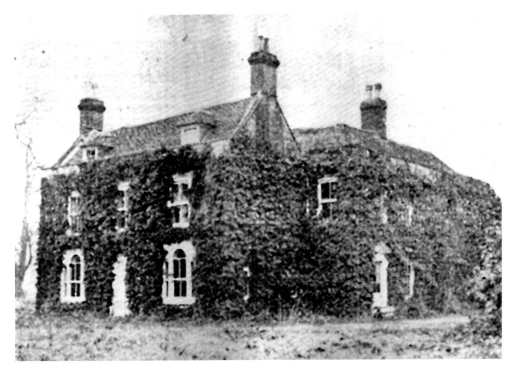

A rare view of Ensbury Manor just before its demolition in 1936. Picture courtesy of the *Daily Echo*, Bournemouth.

Tales are told of maids who, while soundly asleep in their bedrooms, have had the bedclothes snatched from them by an unseen hand. There is also the story of a resident who saw, in the dead of night, a tall figure with a grim, sallow face waiting, alert, in dripping oilskins. The drip of the water as it fell from his oilskins was the more fearful because it made no noise. Nor was there any pool on the floor when the uncanny visitant had departed.

In its abandoned state, Ensbury Manor was certainly a creepy place – 'a typical ghost's playground', as the *Daily Echo* put it. 'Its medley of curiously shaped rooms are mixed up in a bewildering maze. Two staircases with delightful turns and twists add to the puzzle of its riot of nooks and corners. An explorer in the upper apartments is held in a constant state of expectancy.'

In a separate story a few days later, the *Daily Echo* added the following:

There are people living in the Kinson district who, in their young days, were employed at the [Ensbury] Manor house, and they have some curious reminiscences of the place. Stories are told in the village today of a room, which was kept strictly locked, in which some mysterious secret was supposed to be concealed. One Kinson man – he was a boy at the time – remembers spending an evening at the Manor, when he and the butler were the only people in the house. He had gone to keep the butler company. Suddenly a door banged and there was a distinct rustle of clothes as of someone passing the room they were in. The butler said that was always happening.

A CASTLE FULL OF GHOSTS

There was certainly no shortage of strange happenings during his time as manager of Highcliffe Castle, between 1999 and 2004, but the events that unfolded one Saturday morning stand out in Mike Allen's memory. Mike, now retired, was alone in the castle library when he opened the double doors into the conservatory intending to take a photograph of the whole room.

> As the camera flashed, the room seemed to empty of oxygen and atmosphere. It was like a hurricane coming through and it knocked me flying. The doors to the conservatory flew open and the gravel crunched outside as if several people were running through. I sat down and thought, 'this can't be happening'. The next person to see me said I looked as if I had seen a ghost!

The library was the scene of many other strange happenings during Mike's five years in charge, often involving electrical equipment. Light bulbs used to flicker or go out, tools would move around the room and the chained doors at the end would suddenly start rattling.

> One evening we had unplugged all the display cabinet lights, turned the main lights off and locked up. Then someone arrived with a painting for an exhibition we were mounting so I went back in and found that all the lights were back on and the plugs back in their sockets.

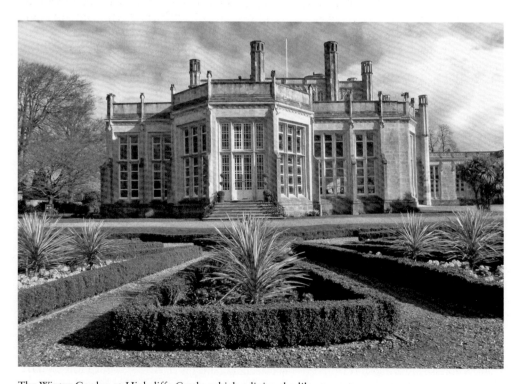

The Winter Garden at Highcliffe Castle, which adjoins the library.

I couldn't believe what was happening but over the next two or three months the same thing happened several more times. I used to check the burglar alarm but there was never any record of anyone having been there. This went on and on and on.

When a paranormal investigation team arrived, the batteries in their cameras and other equipment were drained of power within seconds. 'They didn't take many photographs in the library because they couldn't, and some of their other equipment registered temperature changes,' says Mike. 'They reconvened in the drawing room and the pictures showed three or four orbs over my shoulder.'

On another occasion Mike arrived for the first day of a craft exhibition and was puzzled when a disgruntled exhibitor told him, 'It's a bit petty'. The man was referring to the spotlighting, which he had arranged to point downwards on his stall, only to find next day that it was pointing upwards. 'He assumed that we had moved the lights but we hadn't,' says Mike. 'They had decided to re-set themselves overnight – and against the force of gravity.'

Mike used to have a German Schnauzer dog called Ashley, who always refused to pass through the library. One evening he tried to drag the reluctant pet across the room and Ashley was so frightened that he urinated on the floor.

Another odd phenomenon was the placing of a small number of small, smooth, round stones on the doormat; Mike subsequently learnt that a presence will sometimes leave a stone to say it has been there.

One female visitor to Highcliffe Castle would not walk through the basement, as it made her feel 'uncomfortable and cold'. The paranormal investigators told Mike that they detected the presence of children – and one child in particular who 'did not want to be there and wanted to escape'. 'I told them there were never any children living here but later I remembered that it was a children's home in the early 1950s. Perhaps it has something to do with that,' says Mike. In fact, the home was at the centre of a child abuse investigation that led to both a court case and its closure.

Alison Crocker, a psychic healer from Fordingbridge, believes Highcliffe Castle, which was built in the early nineteenth century, is haunted by ghosts from a number of different time periods. The building was a fire-ravaged ruin when she first visited it as a child, and she found it a scary place. A few years ago she returned to prepare for her part in one of the paranormal investigations that have taken place there.

One of the castle staff took me down to a very creepy basement area. I felt uncomfortable and was very aware of spirit children. I saw some orbs, too. They are tiny balls of light believed to be the first stages of spirit manifestation. While sitting in the gardens, I also saw the image of a tall lady walking towards me. She had dark hair but going grey and was wearing a longish skirt and light sweater. There appeared to be something around her neck like a scarf. She didn't appear to know I was there but I noted immediately her graceful manner and very upright stance. In my head, I kept hearing the year 1927. I wrote down everything I saw and sensed, then went inside to tell one of the staff about it.

One staff member told Alison that it sounded like a description of Dame Nellie Melba, an Australian opera singer who visited the castle in the 1920s. But Mike Allen believes Alison's description of a 'tall elegant lady' sounds more like Mrs Violet Stuart Wortley, the last occupant in its years as a private residence.

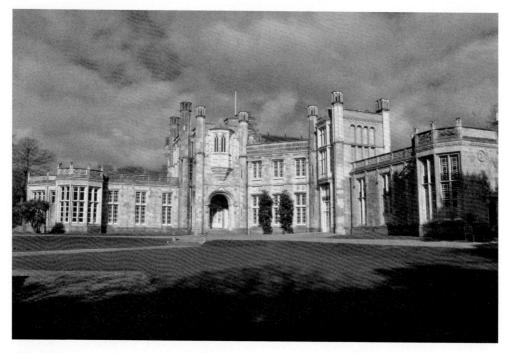

Highcliffe Castle, built in the early nineteenth century, is said to be haunted by ghosts from several time periods.

Alison also saw 'lots of soldier spirits in the trees outside. They were in American uniforms from the Second World War. When I later found out that American soldiers were actually based here, I was blown away.'

There is evidence that Mrs Stuart Wortley herself was aware of hauntings during her time at Highcliffe Castle from 1891-1950. The castle's historian Ian Stevenson, a former *Daily Mirror* journalist, recently showed me a letter that Mrs Stuart Wortley wrote to Shane Leslie in 1947. She told her fellow author, 'Do you remember a visit you paid to Highcliffe when Gladys Martin rented it for a few weeks? You were convinced that you met a ghost in the passage. I think I have since told you that Highcliffe is full of ghosts – not tiresome ones, or mischievous and noisy, but a sort of permeating presence of dead and gone personalities. Felt in the atmosphere but never obtrusive.'

CHAPTER FOUR

HAUNTED HOSTELRIES

THE JERSEY LILY

The television serial *Lillie*, which followed the life of the legendary royal mistress Lillie Langtry, was one of the most popular TV dramas of the 1970s. But as the first instalment hit the screens towards the end of 1978, the Bournemouth love-nest that Edward Prince of Wales (later Edward VII) built for the 'Jersey Lily' in 1877 was experiencing a little drama of its own. The programme was being broadcast across the nation when Pamela Hamilton Howard, owner of the Langtry Manor Hotel in Derby Road, Bournemouth, heard what she described as a 'terrific thud'. Upon further investigation, she found that a tapestry and its ornamental frame had mysteriously 'fallen' to the ground – mysteriously because not only was there no one in the vicinity at the time but the nail from which it had hung on the wall was still firmly in place and the chain which held it was unbroken. 'We had always believed that Lillie made the tapestry and, who knows, her spirit might have been trying to send us a message,' said Pamela.

What that message might have been, no one has suggested. However, Albert White, a minister at the Bath Road Spiritualist Church in Bournemouth, commented at the time, 'It is quite a common occurrence for astral beings to make some gesture, such as knocking down a picture, to show they are aware of what is going on.'

The tapestry incident was not the first 'strange happening' at the Langtry Manor, nor would it be the last. Mike Weatherley, who was the hotel and restaurant's chef for many years, insisted that he 'felt a presence' in the kitchen at 4 p.m. every day. It has been suggested that this was the time when Lillie went in for tea. 'He says he feels it is a female presence,' said Pamela. 'It's not a nasty presence but it's there all the same.'

One guest was frightened to be left alone in a particular room. This had been Lillie Langtry's bedroom and included tiles painted by Lillie herself. There have also been alleged sightings of Edward Prince of Wales in a downstairs room and stories of Lillie's 'ghostly carriage' drawing up the driveway of the house next door in the early hours.

Tara Howard, Pamela's daughter and the present managing director of the Langtry Manor, is an avowed sceptic who tends to dismiss an unexplained sound as a 'creaky floorboard or something', but she admits, 'I do believe that if there was going to be somewhere that had ghosts, this would be it. But I'm sure it would be friendly because the place has a friendly feel. Various people have said they have seen someone sitting in a room and that sort of thing.'

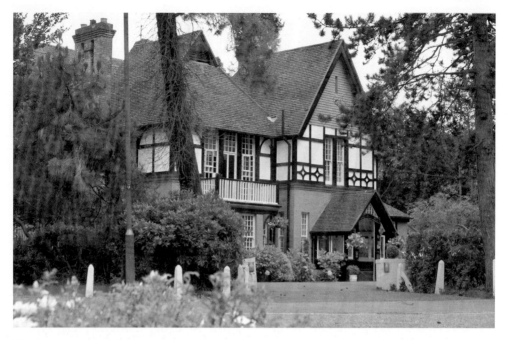

The Langtry Manor Hotel at Bournemouth was built in 1877 by the future Edward VII as a love-nest for his mistress, Lillie Langtry.

THE PHANTOM PIANIST

Demolition and structural alterations are well-known triggers for paranormal activity, and that seems to have been the case at the Crown Hotel in Market Street, Poole. Unexplained noises had been heard there in the past but the events became more varied and more frequent after workmen began converting an old stable into a beat music venue in 1966, and licensee Alan Brown believed that the alterations had disturbed some ghostly energy.

During the renovation work, friends Paul Eeles, Eric Drayman and Malcolm Squire were standing in the courtyard when they heard a single note being played repeatedly on a piano. When Paul, who worked at the Crown, told them it was a ghost, the others thought he was pulling their legs. But when they investigated the hayloft, where the note seemed to be coming from, not only did they find the piano lid closed and no one there but also all the objects that were on the instrument flew off it in front of their eyes. After fleeing the hayloft, they turned to see a 'fluorescent mist' float down the staircase behind them, across the courtyard and into the hotel.

Other happenings reported in the 1960s included the mysterious scattering of workmen's tools in the outbuildings, doors opening and closing themselves, lights flickering on and off, the noise of horses' hooves in the courtyard and the sound of a body being dragged across the floor. Even Mr D. Browne, a sceptical Australian, who set out to prove that the events were all imagined, had to admit there was something strange going on. After painting five crosses on the hayloft door, bolting it and retreating to the courtyard, he looked on in amazement when he saw that the door had opened itself. 'It was the most eerie feeling I have ever had in my life,' he told reporters.

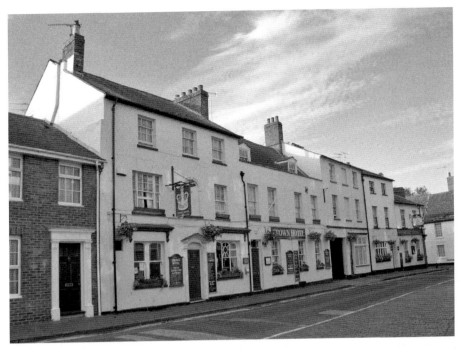

The Crown Hotel in Poole, where structural alterations appear to have set off paranormal activity in 1966.

The 1966 alterations also uncovered a hidden, door-less attic room in the outbuildings. Such secret rooms are often found in pre-Victorian houses that were associated with smugglers and were used for hiding contraband. However, some writers have offered a more sinister explanation in the case of the Crown, suggesting that the room was where a long-dead landlord, too embarrassed to show his deformed twin children in public, reputedly imprisoned them before disposing of their bodies at a later date.

Many more unexplained events have been reported since the 1960s, most notably in 1975, when a milkman refused to deliver to the back door after hearing the screams of panic-stricken children in the courtyard. He was not alone. The landlord's wife said she too had heard such noises in the early morning. Hotel guests reported gusts of cold air in parts of the building.

In 1977 there were fresh reports of horses' hooves and wagon sounds in the courtyard, although by then it was full of parked cars. In 1989 new owners Malcolm and Pat Miller reported that much of the traditional activity was still going on, including lights flickering on and off, balls of light shooting across rooms before disappearing and icy blasts of air. It was also claimed that people outside the hotel had seen the figure of an unidentified woman behind one of the top windows, while inside a young girl in a white nightdress was seen leaning on the banisters.

More recently, a hotel guest noticed that the door of his room was rattling with increasing violence. When he moved towards it, it stopped. Then the handle moved and the door opened but there was no one on the other side. As he went back into the room, a ball of blue light floated around and drifted through the open door and down the hall. Staff had to calm another guest, who claimed that an elderly man he had been talking to in the gents' toilet had simply vanished into thin air.

THE GHOST AT TABLE 28

In August 1975, I wrote a story for the *Evening Echo* about a relief manager who had refused to spend a second night in the Old Thatch at Uddens Cross, Stapehill – 'scared off,' say the locals, 'by things that go clink in the night'. Les Watkinson was too embarrassed to talk to a reporter but customers at the picturesque pub-restaurant on the outskirts of Ferndown were in no doubt about the cause of his sudden departure. Some said he had heard furniture moving around and glasses clinking in the night, others that he had 'seen a ghost'. Mr Watkinson's employers, Whitbread, took the matter seriously enough to replace him with not one but two relief managers so they would not have to sleep alone in the creaky attic rooms beneath the thatched roof.

What Mr Watkinson may not have realised is that he was not the first person to encounter the spooky side of the Old Thatch, a building that dates from 1747 and was originally a lodge to Uddens House, now long-demolished; nor would he be the last. There had long been stories that the place was haunted by an old lady found dead in a rocking chair in the garden many years before. In 1964, a few years after the opening of a restaurant in the building, a newspaper reported that 'crockery and cutlery, laid out on the tables overnight, was found scattered around the floor'. Since then, a succession of managers have reported beer mats falling off the bars, lights switching themselves on, scattered cutlery, falling furniture and a ghostly figure carrying a tray.

In 1972, soon after a forty-four-year-old Polish-born licensee called Jerzy 'George' Dekowski died following a fall down the stairs in which he fractured his skull, staff reported two bizarre and near-identical incidents involving bottles of Cointreau liqueur behind the bar. Speaking in 1975, another former manager, Roy Redfern, recalled, 'I first worked there under Mr Dekowski and within a week or two of his death there were two weird and inexplicable events. Twice in a fortnight Cointreau bottles on the optics shelf behind the bar exploded. On each occasion the glass letter 'U' from the word Cointreau was blown out and both times the letter landed at the feet of a waitress whom Mr Dekowski didn't used to get on with.'

Mr Redfern said that even the suppliers and manufacturers were unable to explain the minor explosions, which had never been known in a Cointreau bottle before. Staff concluded that the letter 'U' was shorthand for 'you' and that the spirit of Mr Dekowski was trying to convey a message to the waitress. The theory was further fuelled by stories that Ray Williams, who was the permanent manager in 1975 and was convalescing at the time of Les Watkinson's brief stay, had held secret séances and succeeded in contacting Mr Dekowski, who revealed that he had 'not finished what he had set out to do'. Yet another story was that on the anniversary of Mr Dekowski's death, Mr Williams himself fell down the stairs and cut his head in the same place as his ill-fated predecessor.

In 1986 the building was badly damaged by a fire but the Old Thatch poltergeist appears to have survived even this. A year or two later, with the premises rebuilt, manager Rusty Garner and his wife complained of finding cutlery scattered on the floor overnight and would not stay there alone. In 1989, the Garners' successors, Paul and Claire Wright and their three children, packed their bags after just eight months, citing ghostly goings-on as one of the reasons. I was again the reporter involved in this story and Mr Wright told me:

There were occasions when glasses would fall off the shelves but the most astounding incident was at Easter when we heard a bang in the bar after going upstairs to bed. I went down and found that three chairs had fallen over onto their backs. The premises were

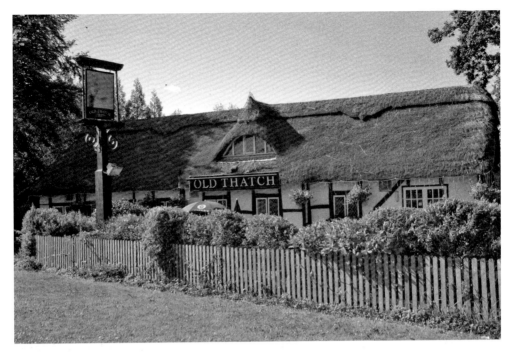

The Old Thatch at Uddens Cross has had recurring poltergeist activity since at least the 1960s.

locked. There was no one else in the building and there is just no normal explanation. The spooky happenings never actually harmed us but having young children, they didn't seem a good thing to live with.

The Wrights even faced a rebellion by their cleaners, who refused to come in at their normal time in the early hours. They complained of seeing lights on as they came up the drive, only to find there were no lights after all. One said she could 'sense something' in the older part of the building.

Kingsley and Kathy Parry have not experienced any ghostly happenings since they took over as tenant landlords in 2006. They do not live on the premises but the barman who does reports nothing untoward either. However, observant diners will notice that although the table numbers include thirteen and go up to thirty-three, there is no longer a table number twenty-eight. This, according to the summary of the Old Thatch's history in the menu folders, is where the ghost of an old lady has 'on numerous occasions' been seen seated in her rocking chair.

THE GHOST WHO CRIED AT CHRISTMAS

Flats now stand on the site once occupied by the Griffin Hotel at Wimborne, which was demolished some years ago but in its heyday was a popular watering hole for those using the nearby railway station and livestock market. It stood near the corner of New Borough Road and Station Road and had a long history of hauntings, which intensified after the old coaching stables were pulled down in the early 1970s. 'A gipsy woman called Mrs Whiteley once warned me that if we pulled down the stables we would be plagued by spirits. She was right,' landlady Eileen Sargeant told me in 1976.

Eileen and her husband, Ronald, a former boxer, described mysterious footprints left in chalk on the bar seats and a 'ghostly voice' which frightened the couple's Alsatian puppy. The pet was sleeping at the top of the stairs when Eileen heard a 'well-spoken female voice' say to it, 'Hello, little fellow. What's your name, then?'

'I hadn't had anything to drink and I came down those stairs like a bat out of hell,' she insisted. Another time she put a tray of glasses on a small table on the landing. Suddenly the table spun round and landed upside down without breaking anything.

According to the Sargeants, the ghostly activity always peaked at Christmas, when they heard a woman crying. 'It sounded liked a woman breaking her heart,' said Eileen, who had also seen the ghost enough times to be able to give a physical description. The apparition was of medium height, medium build, with greying hair and dressed in a beige cardigan with a jumper underneath, a straight brown skirt and lace-up brown shoes.

Much of the action seemed to centre around room number four. Barmaid Sue Greenwood commented:

Sometimes you can't open the wardrobe door. Then you leave it and it flies open by itself. At other times it looks as if someone has jumped on the bed in room four – and that's when it's newly made. Not long after I came here, I and another barmaid called Ruth saw the tail end of a skirt go past the door. Ruth went as white as a sheet. I'm scared stiff of this place. The whole atmosphere in certain places is cold.

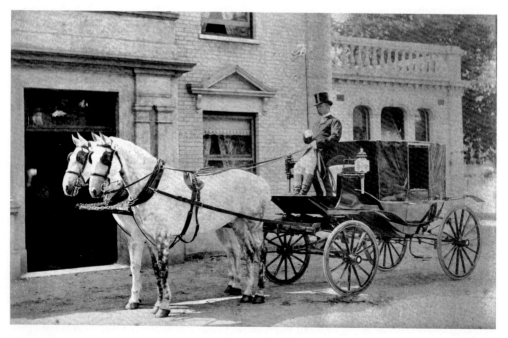

The Griffin Hotel in its heyday as a coaching inn serving Wimborne railway station. Picture courtesy the Priest's House Museum, Wimborne.

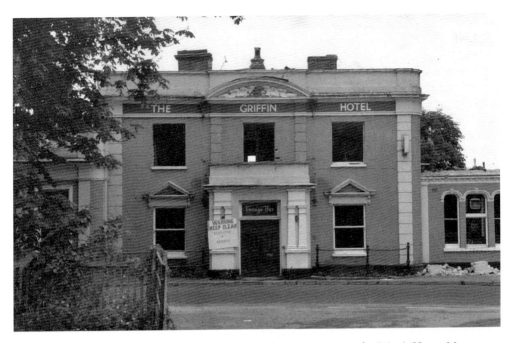

The Griffin Hotel on the eve of its demolition in 1979. Picture courtesy the Priest's House Museum, Wimborne.

Room number four did have an eventful history. At least two people had died in it, a woman had a miscarriage there and Eileen Sargeant once delivered a premature baby in the room.

Rose Cole, who ran the Griffin during the Second World War, was able to add a little more detail. 'She goes backwards and forwards from the bathroom to room four,' she said. 'Then she suddenly vanishes. She's very much like a woman who lived there during the war. That woman's father died in room four.'

ODD FELLOWS AT THE ODDFELLOWS

When Robin and Mary Drake became landlord and landlady of the Oddfellows Arms in Wimborne in September 1980, they knew they were taking over not only one of the oldest pubs in the town but the smallest. What they did not know was that it was also one of the spookiest. It did not take them long to find out. When I visited them for the *Evening Echo* a few weeks later, Robin, aged twenty-four, rolled up his sleeve to reveal the scars of his first and most dramatic encounter with the pub's poltergeist. It happened on only their second night in the building.

'We didn't get to bed until 3 a.m. A bit later we both woke up and felt the bed moving,' twenty-seven-year-old Mary explained. 'When we came to, the bed was literally on the other side of the room, we were underneath it and Robin had grazes and scratches on his arm.'

Next morning a friend who was sleeping in the next room told the couple she had woken up after a dream in which she had heard the sounds of screaming and furniture

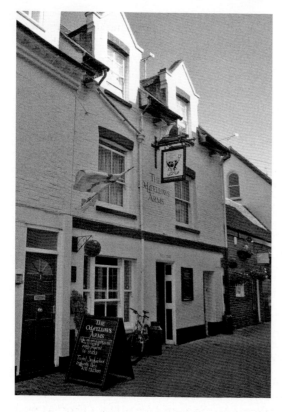

The Oddfellows Arms at Wimborne, where a former landlord and landlady were thrown out of bed by a poltergeist.

being moved around. They informed her she had not been dreaming and that what she had heard was all too real.

Over the next few weeks, several other strange events occurred in the Church Street pub. A barmaid filling bread rolls in the kitchen placed them on a tray before turning away to do something else. When she turned back, she found all the rolls pushed into a heap in one corner of the tray.

On several occasions Robin found that beer barrels had mysteriously disconnected themselves. Fifteen or twenty minutes after they went to bed each night, he and Mary heard footsteps which seemed to be coming from the stairs. Robin wondered if the poltergeist activity was connected to an ornamental brass bell which bore the model of a dog in a crouching position. The bell, thought to be in the exact centre of the ancient building, was rung by pulling a chain. On two occasions Robin inadvertently broke the chain and both times ghostly incidents quickly followed.

Despite the violence of the bed-moving incident, the couple concluded that the ghost was benevolent. 'Before we came here, I didn't believe in such things but I certainly do now,' said Robin. 'There is definitely something here but I think it's trying to help us. We have left the bed where the poltergeist put it and we haven't had any more trouble on that score.'

As the Drakes subsequently discovered, they were not the first licensees to experience strange happenings at the Oddfellows, nor were they to be the last. Linda Flower was unaware of Robin and Mary's experiences when she began her seven years as licensee in about 1995. In fact, she was unaware of it until I told her about it in 2006, although she had heard another tale of a former landlord who spent every night sleeping on a window seat in the bar because he was too frightened to go upstairs. Within three or four months of moving in, Linda had the first of her own ghostly experiences. 'Soon after I arrived, a child ghost began turning my electrical switches on and off,' she said. 'It had to be a small child because he or she couldn't reach higher than about five feet and only touched the lower row of switches. I would turn everything off before going to bed. Then in the morning I would get up to find everything switched on.'

Eventually Linda told her invisible guest, 'You and I get on really well but will you stop f***ing with my electricity because I won't be able to afford the bill!' That night, to her amazement, everything was mysteriously turned off – including things that should have stayed on, such as the refrigerator, freezer, beer taps and lights. From this moment on, there was no further interference with the pub's electricity supply.

There was, however, an equally strange sequel to these mysterious events. 'One day I mentioned the word "exorcism" in the bar and three or four bottles of wine came out off the top shelf and landed on the floor next to me,' she said.

THE GHOSTLY BARMAN

The King's Arms Hotel in Bleke Street, Shaftesbury, has a long history and is said to have been built from stone 'robbed' from the ruins of Shaftesbury Abbey following the dissolution of the monasteries by Henry VIII. In 1681, the inn was named in a Treasury report into corruption after two customs officers from Poole discovered twenty-two packets of smuggled cloth there – and were bribed to ignore the find.

Almost inevitably, considering the hostelry's age, the King's Arms has a ghost as well as a past, and former landlord John Liddy told me in 2006:

> I have not seen him myself but I know people who have. One night, after the pub had closed, I was talking to a customer in the bar and he suddenly froze. I asked him what was up and he said he had just seen somebody walk past. I couldn't see it but he described it as a misty, grey figure strolling through the bar. It went through the wall where the toilets are now, which would have been the coaching arch in days gone by.

John Liddy also described how, in the days when gas bottles were kept in the cellar, he would often find that the gas had been mysteriously turned off. 'A couple of days later, you would find the same thing again,' he said. 'The cellar is always kept locked, and when you are the only one with a key, it's hard to find any other explanation.'

THE SHIP IN THE NIGHT

Landlord Mark Tilbrook's daughter Natalie was only about fourteen when she first encountered the ghost of Shaftesbury's Ship Inn, which stands just across the road from the King's Arms. The building is just as old as its haunted neighbour but it has been a pub for a much shorter time. 'It only became a pub in 1937 – before that it was a doctor's surgery and what's now the public bar was the dispensary,' says Mark. 'I believe that the lounge bar was a row of three cottages.'

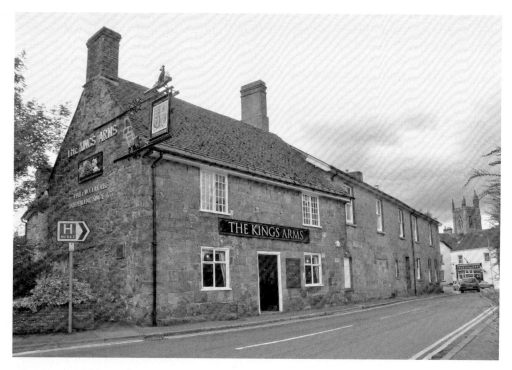

The King's Arms at Shaftesbury, where gas bottles in the cellar were mysteriously turned off.

Natalie's experience occurred in 2003, within a year of her father's appointment as the licensee. On the night in question, she had all the windows of her room closed when she went to bed yet for some reason the metallic blinds inside the windows were rattling. Then she felt a presence on the steps up to her bed. 'She very politely told it that if it was going to do something, would it please get on and do it, and if not, would it go away so she could get some sleep,' says Mark.

The ghost proved obedient and left the teenager in peace. But it was not to be its last intrusion and six years later things still occasionally happen at the Ship. At midnight one night, after the customers had gone home and Mark and former barmaid Gemma Spinney were clearing up, there was a sudden and dramatic temperature drop in the bar. 'It was in the middle of winter three or four years ago and the central heating was on full blast,' Mark recalls. 'Suddenly the temperature plummeted. I never feel the cold but I was so cold that I got goosebumps. Then we heard a crash coming from near the cellar but there was no evidence that anything had fallen down. The coldness lasted about ten minutes. I've been told that customers have experienced similar coldness before I got here.'

On several occasions objects – such as a tin of baked beans and plastic boxes – have fallen off perfectly level shelves for no obvious reason, though no damage has ever been caused. One employee, working a day shift when Mark was out for the day, became convinced that his boss was at home after all, as he could hear someone 'running around' upstairs. 'They were quite spooked when I walked through the door,' says Mark.

He adds that 'these things still happen from time to time and I would welcome an investigation into it. No one has actually seen a ghost but a couple of years ago barman Darren Burmeister saw a black dog in the lounge area, although we don't have a dog and dogs aren't allowed in there.'

THE GHOST OF GALLOWS CLOSE

Perhaps the greatest claim to fame of the Horns Inn at Dudsbury, West Parley, is that it once numbered the Kray twins among its customers. The infamous gangland crooks from London's East End used to stay at the nearby Dudsbury (now the River Park) and would bring their 'more discerning customers' to the Horns. Many of the Horns' customers also claim to have seen the ghost of an old lady dressed in an old-fashioned servant's uniform of black full skirt, headscarf and white pinafore.

'She's about 5ft 2in tall and walks up Gallows Close and along the original back wall of the pub, which is now the corridor between the bar and restaurant,' Vikki Iddon, the licensee's daughter, told me in 2004. Vikki said she had seen the ghost herself eight or nine times. 'She can be a bit of a prankster who lets us know when she doesn't like something. She has taken a few light bulbs out and thrown them across the room,' Vikki added.

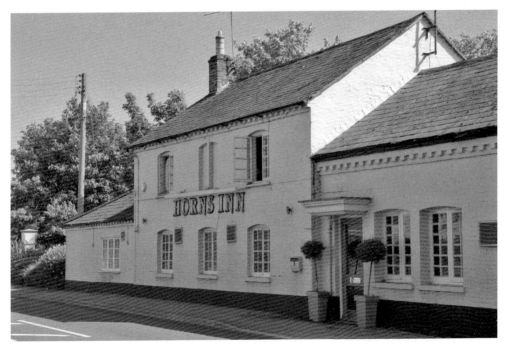

The Horns Inn at Dudsbury, where many customers claim to have seen a ghost in servant's uniform.

CHAPTER FIVE

GHOSTS OF TOWN AND COUNTRY

THE DURWESTON POLTERGEIST

The white-walled, semi-detached cottages high on the hill above the village of Durweston, near Blandford, can be seen for miles around and have been a familiar landmark for 160 years. Yet few of those who travel along the Stour Valley below know of the strange goings-on that occurred there more than a century ago. They were happenings, which, as *The Western Gazette* reported on 11 January 1895, sparked 'considerable excitement' in Durweston 'in consequence of the supposition that one of its cottages is haunted'.

At that time the cottages, which adjoin a wood, were owned by Viscount Portman and one half of the building was occupied by a widow, Mrs Best, her grown-up daughter and two little orphan girls, Annie Cleave, aged twelve or thirteen, and her sister, Gertie, aged four. Mrs Best, aged about sixty, was described by the *Western Gazette* as a 'most respectable woman, of a quiet, inoffensive disposition, and on good terms with her neighbours and the village generally'. The rector of Durweston, the Revd W. M. Anderson, described her as 'an earnest Christian woman, who bears perhaps the highest character in the village'. The little girls had been boarded out to Mrs Best by the Honourable Mrs Pitt, of nearby Steepleton. Annie was not in the best of health. A doctor later described her as being 'of a markedly consumptive tendency' and 'hysterical'. Another sister, Lizzie, two years Annie's senior, had already died of consumption, one of the great killers of the Victorian age. The disease is better known today as tuberculosis.

The disturbances that caused such a stir began 13 December 1894, when Mrs Best became puzzled by the faint sounds of knocking and scratching in various parts of the house. The strange noises were repeated several times over the next few days, gradually increasing in loudness until even Lord Portman's gamekeeper, Mr Newman, who lived in the adjoining house, could also hear them. The village blacksmith said the sounds were 'as heavy as sledgehammer blows'. There was also one uncorroborated report that Annie had seen a 'queer animal with green head, green eyes and a big bushy tail, sitting up and pulling her doll to pieces with its paws'. Gertie apparently also saw it when Annie called her.

As December wore on, the strange noises were succeeded by a series of even more bizarre occurrences. Mrs Best was especially startled when a number of stones came flying through the windows, breaking the glass and then returning of their own

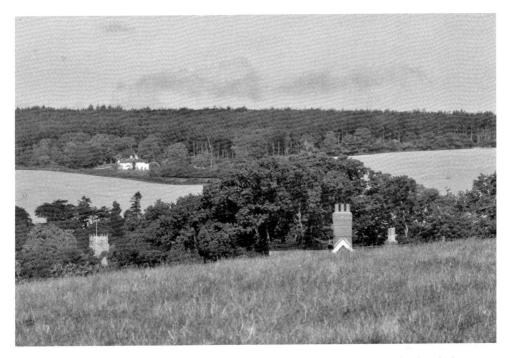

The white cottage at Norton, high on a hill overlooking Durweston, is a familiar landmark that can be seen for miles around. It was the scene of sustained poltergeist activity in 1894-95.

volition through the round holes they had made in the glass. Neighbours carried out a thorough search of the surrounding area in case someone was playing tricks on Mrs Best but they could not find so much as a footprint. On 18 December, Annie Cleave reported seeing a boot come out of the garden plot and strike the back door, leaving a muddy mark. Mr Newman was then called in. He later told an investigator from the Psychical Research Society, Mr Westlake, 'I went into Mrs Best's, and I saw a bead strike the window; and then soon after, a big blue bead struck the window but did not break it. Then I sat down in the chair and said, "You're a coward, you're a coward; why don't you throw money?"'

At this point, events took an even stranger turn. Mr Newman recalled that he was looking at the door to the garden, which was wide open leaving a space of about fifteen inches between it and the inner wall, when he saw a 'quantity of little shells' coming from behind the door.

They came round the door from a height of about five feet. They came one at a time at intervals varying from half-a-minute to a minute. They came very slowly and when they hit me I could hardly feel them. With the shells came two thimbles. They came so slowly that in the ordinary way they would have dropped long before they reached me. They came from a point, some, I think a trifle higher, and some no higher, than my head. Both the thimbles struck my hat. Some [of the shells] missed my head and went just past and fell down slantingwise, not as if suddenly dropped. Those that struck me fell straight down.

The next object to come through the air was a slate-pencil, about two-and-half inches long, which came from behind Mr Newman at an angle and landed in a bowl on the pantry floor. Then a hasp – 'like the hasp of a glove' – dropped into the gamekeeper's lap from somewhere above the level of his head. Finally the woman's boot, which had lain outside the door since the earlier incident, began moving a foot above the ground towards Mr Newman and landed softly beside him. Mrs Best threw the item of footwear – described as 'an old, dirty boot from off the garden plot' – outside. The gamekeeper followed, putting his foot on it and defiantly announcing, 'I defy anything to move this boot'.

'Just as I stepped off, it rose up behind me and knocked my hat off; there was no-one behind me,' said the incredulous Mr Newman who, throughout this episode, was accompanied in the room by both Annie and Gertie as well as Mrs Best. 'The boot and the hat fell down together.'

A few days later Mrs Best and her foster children moved into Mr Newman's cottage, where they were twice visited by Mr Anderson, who was hoping to witness the phenomena. On his first visit on 4 January nothing happened but when the rector returned with the village schoolmaster, Mr Sheppard, on 10 January, the poltergeist wasted little time in making itself known.

Following the two men's arrival, Mrs Best put the two girls to bed and lay on the bed with them with her head at the opposite end. When loud rappings were heard on the walls in different parts of the room, Mr Sheppard went outside to make sure no one was playing tricks while Mr Anderson remained in the bedroom, which was lit by a small hand-lamp on the washstand. The rector noted later:

> I put my ear and hand to the wall but could not detect any vibration; but when resting my hand on the rail at the bottom of the bed, I could distinctly feel a vibration, varying according to the loudness of the knocking… I searched the room and the house, also Mrs Best's house, from top to bottom. Occasionally there was a noise on the wall, as if someone were scratching with their nails. This scratching also appeared to be produced on the mattress of the bed, although I am sure it was not produced by any of the three occupants of the bed, as I could see their hands and watched them very closely all the time.

Mr Anderson observed that to start with the rappings frequently stopped when he came into the room but after a short time his presence made no difference. The sounds went on, 'loud and continuous', for much of the night. At 2.15 a.m., Mr Sheppard imaginatively suggested asking the 'agency' if it would write any communication on a slate. It was invited to deliver a specified number of raps for an affirmative and, remarkably, did so. This was not just any old poltergeist but clearly one with intelligence. It was also patient enough to wait for a slate and pencil to be fetched from Mrs Best's house and intelligent enough to respond to a series of questions as to where the slate should be placed. 'Every conceivable place in the room was suggested one after the other,' said the rector, 'but the right number of raps was not given, but a short, sharp knock, which seemed always to be given for a negative. We almost gave up at this point until, as an afterthought, I suggested the window-sill, which was at once accepted.'

Responding to another series of questions, the poltergeist indicated that only Mrs Best and the two girls were to remain in the room and the light was to be removed. The others made their way to the foot of the stairs but the bedroom door was left wide open. Only fifteen seconds had elapsed when, in almost pitch darkness and 'amid perfect silence', they heard the sound of the pencil scratching on the slate. Mrs Best was heard to give a 'suppressed groan'. The signal agreed to indicate that the writing had finished was four sharp raps, and at the very moment that these were delivered, the sound of the pencil dropping on the slate was also heard, followed immediately by the screaming call of 'Come!' from Mrs Best.

'I was in the room instantly, the whole thing taking less time than it would take to read this description,' said Mr Anderson. 'The light showed some unmeaning scratches on the slate. We asked for something legible, which was promised in the usual way.'

Mrs Best reluctantly agreed to repeat the performance on condition that the rector stayed on the stairs. This time the presence produced a 'flourish' on the slate – curves that were 'beautifully drawn' with firm, bold lines such as no child could produce'. When the exercise was repeated a third and a fourth time, the words 'MONY' and then 'GARDEN' appeared on the slate. Both Mrs Best and Gertie were illiterate. Annie could write, but Mr Anderson was utterly convinced that no one had moved in the bed – which was 4 or 5ft from the window sill – let alone left it; Mrs Best offered to take a solemn oath confirming this in case anyone should doubt it. There being no other rapping, the witnesses left the gamekeeper's cottage at 2.50 a.m. A subsequent search of the garden failed to produce any money.

Previous accounts of the events at Norton suggest that the orphan girls were subsequently sent to stay at a house in the main part of Durweston, where the strange activities continued. While researching for this book, I was given photocopies of two handwritten statements which not only confirm this but add a great deal of detail. The dates given in an account by Fred Cross suggest that the girls came to stay with his family on Christmas Day 1894 but that nothing unusual occurred until they had been back to Norton for one night in early January. On their first night back with the Cross family, a 'strange scratching sound' was heard from their room. At first the host family thought it was a bird but then plaster from the walls and ceiling began to fall on the children's heads. The frightened girls were moved to another room, but the next night the scratching began again and continued even when Fred remained in the room with a light. After a few slight taps the next morning, nothing more was heard until 15 January. That evening, with the girls in bed upstairs, Fred and his mother and sister heard several taps in quick succession. He recalled:

I at once went to the children, finding them all asleep, although a loud knock after I got into the room awoke the eldest orphan. The knocks being repeated, we sent for a few friends to come and hear the noises. The eldest orphan, while dressing, awoke the little one. I gave her several questions to ask the agency (as it would not reply to anyone else), a large number of which were answered by an agreed number of knocks. There was no one except the small child (who was still in bed) within a distance of at least five feet from the spot where the knocks came from, except when it hit the door against which I was standing. A light was burning all the time and Mr Sheppard, our schoolmaster, was in the room when the last of the questions was answered.

The rappings continued 'at intervals' until just after midnight, the last knock coinciding with the arrival of the rector. There were no noises the following night, but on 17 January events took an even more extraordinary turn. 'As soon as I was in bed, the knocking began again, keeping time with any tune which was well-known by the children,' said

Fred. 'I asked for several comic, school and sacred songs, which were all answered by raps on the head of the bedstead for each single note. The only tune we asked for which was not rapped out was The British Grenadiers.'

Fred added that a light was burning throughout and, to make sure that neither child was doing the knocking, he held their hands throughout. The knocking ceased just after midnight but began again next morning, when requested songs were again rapped out. Gertie Cleave was taken away that afternoon, Annie the following Monday. Other sources confirm that the sisters were separated at this point. What happened to Gertie is unknown but Annie initially went to stay with a woman at Iwerne Minster. There the disturbances resumed. Noises were heard, mostly on the outer walls of the house, a large stone was thrown at the porch roof and snowdrops were dug from the garden and flung about. On 7 March 1895, Miss W. H. Mason, a local government inspector of boarded-out children, took Annie to stay in her flat in London for a week. Official records suggest that 'no disturbance worth recording' took place there, although the other handwritten account – which is unsigned and was clearly written many years later – claims Annie was found to have 'highly developed powers as a medium'. Sadly, all accounts agree that the unfortunate girl died soon after of consumption.

More on this kind of phenomenon appears in the section on The Winton Poltergeist.

TERROR ON THE EVENING TRAIN

Margaret Mortimore was entirely alone as she began her short train journey from Wareham to Poole at dusk on a July evening in 1947. The carriage was dimly lit by a single light bulb, but after some minutes Ms Mortimore became aware of what she described as 'a presence'. 'At the far corner of the carriage was a woman seated with her back to the engine, facing directly towards me,' she later wrote in an article for *Fate* magazine. She continued:

> Fighting against panic, I tried in vain to explain what I saw. As I watched, the woman rose and walked past me. She was enveloped from head to foot in black, flowing robes, like the apparel of a nun, wrapped over her head like a cowl and stretching to the floor. She had a dead-white face and terrible, staring eyes that were fixed on me with an expression of burning malice. She stood with a white hand on the door handle. She moved the other hand in a beckoning gesture, motioning me towards the door. I realised, with a sense of cold horror and fascination, that she wanted me to step out of the speeding train. I was frozen to my seat but I felt something drawing me toward the door. There seemed to be a dark, urgent and magnetic force in the woman's gesture, which I had to fight with all my strength to resist. I solemnly believe that in another few moments I would have obeyed the summons, but then I felt the train slowing. I did not actually see the woman go but she was not on the platform and the ticket-collector had not seen her.

Only a small minority of incidents feature apparitions that appear to have any malicious intent but this is clearly one of them. Ms Mortimore speculated that her silent companion was the ghost of someone who had jumped from the train at some time in the past and had now returned to lure other travellers to their deaths.

Although Ms Mortimore alighted at Poole station, she appears to have been unaware that this location had a ghost of its own – a young woman in a long white dress, which witnesses have likened to a Victorian wedding gown. The spectral bride – if bride she is – also has white gloves on her hands, dark hair tied up on her head and appears to be in a big hurry to get somewhere.

According to Poole ghost author Julie Harwood, the Poole High Street level crossing, a little further along the line towards Bournemouth, is the scene of yet another railway haunting. Many times in the 1940s, signalmen often saw a male figure staring up the line from the middle of the track. It happened so often that they gave him a nickname – 'Crossing Cuthbert'. But whenever they investigated, there was no one there. He was never seen from ground level and has not been seen at all since 1949.

THE GHOST THAT CAUSED AN ACCIDENT

It was 5.30 a.m. on a cold, frosty morning in February 1972 when thirty-year-old Robin Legg set off for work on his bicycle. He lived in Berrans Avenue, Kinson, on the outskirts of Bournemouth and his route took him along Millhams Road to the village of Longham. 'I had just got to the end of the road,' he said, 'when suddenly, there in the beam of my cycle lamp, was a greyish figure. I could see no face but distinctly made out some sort of cape which was flapping about. It was moving across the road towards some grassland at about normal walking speed. As it was going directly on my path, I jammed on my brakes hard. The road was icy, the bike slipped from under me and I finished up on my backside on the ground. By the time I looked again, the figure had gone.'

When he came home from work and told the tale, Robin's wife, Linda, could not stop laughing. But her husband was less amused. 'He was really shocked and frightened,' she told *Bournemouth Times* reporter David Haith when the couple finally went public on the incident several months later. 'He's quite serious and he is not the type to imagine things.'

At the time of his mishap, Robin was unaware of other ghostly sightings at Longham – such as the one by the young son of a policeman in November 1971. The boy was found terrified and screaming in his garden and explained that he had seen 'a lady in a long white dress'. The sighting might have been dismissed as the product of a child's over-active imagination had not corroborative evidence then begun to appear. When the youngster's experience was related in one of the Longham pubs, a customer said that his neighbour, while burning rubbish in his garden one evening, had seen the figure of a woman in a long white dress and wearing a bonnet. He found the experience so frightening that he had refused to venture into the garden after dark ever since.

Ann Jorgensen, who described these incidents in a letter to the *Evening Echo* in January 1972, added that as a child she too had been told about 'a lady who haunted the banks of the Stour at Longham'. Mrs Jorgensen's letter, in turn, prompted Gene Young to recall her experience as a six year old at Bear Cross, barely half-a-mile from Longham. 'As a small child I lived with my grandparents, Mr and Mrs Harry Penny, in one of the two cottages that used to stand on the Wimborne Road just above the Bear Cross Hotel,' Mrs Young wrote. 'I was coming downstairs one day when I saw the old lady exactly as described on the staircase. When I told my grandmother, she told me it was an old lady named Mrs Gridger, who had lived in the house many years before.'

TOWN HALL HAUNTINGS

With an age difference of almost sixty years, the elderly cleaner and the teenage disc jockey probably had very little in common. But on one thing they certainly agreed – that Bournemouth Town Hall was haunted, and they were not the only ones who thought so.

In 1980, part-time cleaner Tom Webb, aged seventy-five, was working on the third floor of the town hall when a shadowy figure drifted towards him.

> I had this eerie feeling, looked round and saw this dark shape moving towards me. It stopped only about 6ft away and I felt a blast of very cold air. I could see plainly that it was a man dressed in eastern clothes with a turban. I could see that his face was a kind of mahogany colour and he had a beard. Then, after a few seconds, he faded away like a film image. I nearly jumped out of my skin and rushed down to the ground floor. I went so fast that my feet didn't touch the steps. Now I'm uneasy about going to the third floor in case the ghost is about.

Town hall attendant Fred Killick, aged sixty-four, also had an encounter with the paranormal but his occurred when he was checking the telephone switchboard restroom in the basement. Hearing footsteps in the corridor outside, he dashed out to see who was there – but found no one. 'Nobody was about, I'm certain of that,' he said. 'I didn't believe in this ghost business but now I'm not so sure.'

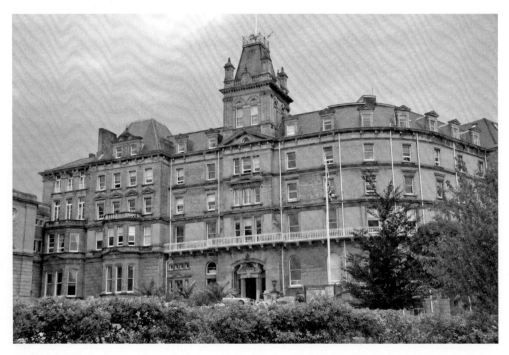

An elderly cleaner and a teenaged disc jockey were among those who agreed that Bournemouth Town Hall was haunted.

Disc jockey Nick Dunford, aged eighteen, described what happened as he and his helper, Mark Loader, were packing up their equipment following one of the dances which were held in the town hall around 1980.

> We heard these heavy clunking footsteps by the gents' toilet near the entrance but could find nobody there. Then we kept hearing the same footsteps all over the hall and every time we walked to the spot the sounds came from, they would restart at another place. We were following them for fifteen minutes. We were pretty worried. We searched the place thoroughly and we're sure nobody was about. I'm sure it was a ghost. It was so very real yet somehow unreal. We heard the footsteps the next week too but we didn't follow them that time.

Yet another witness was the promoter of the disco, John Ratcliff, aged thirty-nine. He said:

> I went into the hall before the others arrived to check that everything was ready. Suddenly I heard this distant thudding sound of footsteps which moved across the hall. I walked towards the sound but there was nobody there. I know it's childish to be frightened and normally I'd take on ten men if they set on me. But this was different. I got out of the place very quickly.

The elegant building has not always been the town hall and the late Dick Sheppard, who was the council's information officer in 1980, believed its earlier history offered the most likely explanation for the hauntings. The building began life in 1885 as the Mont Dore Hotel, a luxury establishment for guests with tuberculosis and other chest ailments. It became a military hospital in the First World War before being taken over by Bournemouth Borough Council in 1921.

Dick Sheppard, who also had a special interest in ghosts, believed the town hall phantom was the ghost of an Indian soldier from the First World War, who died in the building when it was a military convalescent home. A second explanation was that the 'misty figure' seen on the third and fourth floors was the ghost of a person who had committed suicide by throwing himself off the building some years earlier. Dick added that one member of staff claimed to have been tapped on the shoulder 'by some unseen force'.

THE WINTON POLTERGEIST

When window-cleaner Charles Burden set off for work as usual on Friday 14 August 1981, he could not have imagined that his family's normally peaceful existence was about to be shattered. There was one early sign that everything was not as it should be when, at 5 a.m., the family's thirteen-year-old black Labrador, Panda, began howling. Mr Burden ignored it, assuming that the animal had been disturbed by cats. It did not occur to him that Panda was reacting to some strange supernatural power – a power that would shortly throw the household into turmoil and plunge them into the media spotlight on an international scale.

Living with Mr Burden at 37 Abbott Road, Winton, Bournemouth, were his wife, Kathy, who was forty-five and suffered from Huntington's chorea (at the time it was thought she had multiple sclerosis), their seventeen-year-old adopted daughter, Debbie, who worked as an auxiliary nurse, and their retarded foster son, Bradley, who was eight.

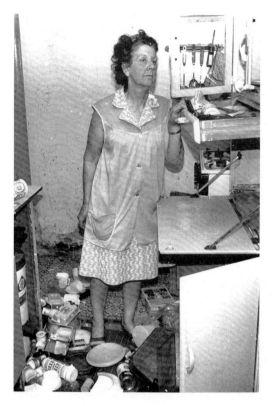

Kathy Burden surveys the poltergeist's work in her kitchen. Photo by Duncan Lee, *Evening Echo*, Bournemouth.

Only Mrs Burden and Bradley were in the seventy-year-old detached house at 9 a.m. when vases and ornaments started flying across rooms and crockery began to jump off shelves.

'I was upstairs making the beds when I heard something downstairs,' Mrs Burden told my *Evening Echo* colleague Chris Adamson later. 'It was two bottles of squash falling off a shelf in the kitchen. Then the table in the hall, with flowers on it, fell over. Everything was falling around. The television went up and fell over and all the things on the top fell off.'

The destruction continued for an hour. Neighbours rushed round in response to Mrs Burden's cries for help. Her husband was sent for and arrived home at 9.30 a.m. He was immediately aware of a strange atmosphere. He described the house as 'very cold' and himself as 'very frightened'. He decided to call the police but as he lifted the receiver, it was wrenched from his hand by an invisible force. Then a large paraffin heater suddenly flew from one side of the hall to the other and crashed into the wall. The table on which the telephone stood began to shake, throwing off a flowerpot and other objects. In the lounge, the television toppled onto its screen and a heavy gas fire fell forward from the grate.

Mr Burden eventually succeeded in contacting the police and the first two officers to arrive were able to confirm the events. Sgt Alan Woods estimated the temperature drop at 10-15° or more. PC Graham Joyce said he heard Mrs Burden cry out that it was getting cold again. Then there was a terrific crash in the kitchen.

'There was a hell of a bang; then, as I came in, the kitchen cabinet was falling to the ground,' said PC Joyce. 'It was really eerie. There is no logical explanation for it. I've never believed these sort of things before but this was weird.'

The kitchen cabinet had tipped its entire contents on to the floor. On police advice, a priest was sent for. Dr Frederick Oliver, assistant at St Alban's Church, Bournemouth, arrived at noon to conduct a service of exorcism. The *Evening Echo* reported:

Dr Oliver, a graduate from Yale and London Universities, asked everyone to be quiet and as the house became peaceful for the first time yesterday, he prayed for the spirits to go away. After calling on the evil spirits to leave the house, he asked everyone to join in the Lord's Prayer. Satisfied that there would be no further trouble, Dr Oliver talked about the forces of evil that he felt coming from the room. 'There is something evil still in the house but I do not think it will manifest itself again,' he said.

According to the Burdens' only natural daughter, Mrs Noreen Penfold, the priest also sprinkled 'holy water' in the house, only to find that it came back in his face. Later that day, several people took part in a séance at 37 Abbott Road. They included Mrs Penfold, who claimed to be clairvoyant, fifty-two-year-old Mrs Marie Nadin, who lived nearby in a house formerly occupied by the Burdens, and David Haith, a *Bournemouth Times* reporter who had a special interest in the paranormal. In his report the following week, Haith described how Mrs Nadin began 'shaking and mumbling'.

'Seated with two mediums and others round a greenhouse table,' he wrote, 'I suddenly saw Mrs Nadin take on a tortured expression and cry out, "Go away". Then one medium comforted her and asked the spirit – thought to be of a neighbour who hanged himself – to "join with them in the brighter world". After several minutes, Mrs Nadin shuddered and came out of the trance and rested her head on the table, exhausted.'

Afterwards, Mrs Nadin told Haith, 'I was frightened. I felt that someone was making me do what I didn't want to do. There was something within me that wasn't me. But towards the end everything was getting lighter. Nothing like this has ever happened to me before. I've never thought of myself as a medium.'

The night of 14 August 1981 was peaceful and it began to appear that Dr Oliver's belief that the 'evil' would not manifest itself again might be justified. But at 9 o'clock the following morning, the destruction began again. Debbie, who was still in bed, said later, 'My mother and Bradley were downstairs when a milk bottle crashed to the floor. Then, when I was downstairs, all the things on the television and a table fell off and the television fell over. It was only when Bradley and Mum went across the road that things stopped happening.'

There was more drama later in the morning and again it was witnessed by outsiders. A social worker described how she was in the kitchen helping to make a pot of tea when things began to move around. Then, like the policemen a day earlier, she watched in amazement as a cabinet laden with food and crockery crashed to the ground. 'Things were crashing around and there was no explanation for it. Things were flying past us but not at us. They were whizzing round with terrific force,' she said.

For the second day running, a churchman was sent for. This time the man chosen was Mr Albert White of the Bath Road Spiritualist Church in Bournemouth, who decided that another séance was in order. It was conducted in the lounge and involved eight people sitting around a table and attempting to communicate with the spirit world. David Haith was present again and the participants also included Debbie and Bradley. Reporting that this time it was Debbie's turn to find herself 'taken over', Haith went on:

> One medium present clairvoyantly gave the surname of a neighbour who was hanged and mumbled: 'I didn't do it. I wouldn't do it,' and clutched his neck as if in pain. Then came the words: 'It's a child. It's all fun to them. Ian comes to play'. Bradley was then asked: 'Who is Ian?' And he replied: 'My friend'. It was then that Debbie began shaking and suddenly said: 'He's still here'. Then she giggled in a child's voice.

Kathy Burden was not present at this second séance but afterwards she and her husband revealed that Bradley did indeed have an imaginary playmate called Ian. The boy would talk to him in the garden and offer him a kick of his football or a ride on his bike, but the couple were not worried by this. When they asked who he was talking to he would say, 'just somebody'.

Describing her feelings during the séance, Debbie told reporters:

I suddenly felt cold. It kind of crept up from my feet. It was cold under the table and then my breathing got clearer and deeper. I felt something inside my stomach – I had this sharp feeling above my tummy – but when the medium questioned me I started giggling and went shy. I couldn't say anything because I felt shy. I didn't know what was going on but I felt like a child and wanted to laugh. Then Ian went through the medium and was able to speak to us.

Charles Burden said:

This spirit called to Bradley and laughed with him. He told us that he was nine years old and he was working through our daughter, Deborah. We pictured him as being fair-haired. He spoke through the medium in a child's voice and said he was doing all these things for fun but he wouldn't tell us about himself. It was very strange. I have never believed in this sort of thing before but I will believe in it now.

The mediums advised the Burdens to leave the house for four days. Charles moved to a boarding house, his wife went to stay with a friend at Portsmouth, Debbie stayed with neighbours and Bradley stayed with Noreen Penfold at West Howe and later at a nearby children's home.

By this time the family and their experiences had become headline news. The *Daily Mirror* even arranged for a reporter and photographer to spend two days and nights in the deserted house, complete with an elaborate arrangement of cameras and tripwires. At one point the cameras were activated but the visitor turned out to be not a wandering spirit but a wandering cat. The creature went on to bite reporter Alister Martin as he brandished the crucifix given to him by Charles Burden for protection. In the excitement, the photographer cut his hand on a piece of broken glass on the floor. Apart from that, Martin reported, all was quiet at 37 Abbott Road.

Another visitor to the abandoned house was Miriam Jeffreys, from Southampton, who claimed to have been told by a white witch that she had special powers. She arrived, as the *Evening Echo* put it, 'carrying a Bible and wooden cross and clothed in a shining white dress, like an avenging angel'. Her request to meet Bradley was turned down by Mr Burden but he allowed her inside the house and afterwards reported that she 'talked a lot of sense'. After placing pictures of Kathy, Debbie and Bradley between the pages of her leather-bound Bible, she said there was now no reason why the family could not return to their home.

The Burdens and the authorities were inundated with press inquiries and offers of help from mediums and other psychic specialists. One approach to the Dorset Police came from a woman said to be 'high up in Government circles', who expressed her willingness to help with the Abbott Road situation as long as there was no risk of publicity. A senior Dorset officer, who was involved in the Winton case, recalled later:

I replied that the Press were already having a field day and 'no publicity' was the last thing I could guarantee. What interested me was that the woman also asked if there was a mentally retarded or handicapped child in the house. I replied that there was not and it was only later that I learned that the family had a foster son who was retarded.

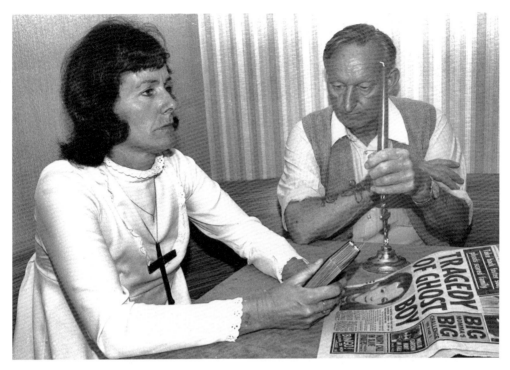

Miriam Jeffreys, who claimed to have 'special powers', with Charles Burden. Photograph by Duncan Lee, *Evening Echo*, Bournemouth.

As the story reached an audience of millions, speculation on the cause of the poltergeist activity became rife. Students of the paranormal noted that on the day before the opening events of the Abbott Road drama, many people in the same area of Winton had reported seeing a 'huge, rumbling UFO' fly overhead. Did this constitute evidence to support the theory that ghosts and UFOs were in some way linked? A member of the Society for Psychical Research observed that the Abbott Road case was similar to that of the Enfield poltergeist, which famously plagued a family in their council house for fourteen months between 1977 and 1979. At the centre of the Enfield case, which involved a wide range of paranormal phenomena witnessed by a number of reliable witnesses and even a professional photographer's camera, was an eleven-year-old girl. It has long been recognised that a high proportion of such cases involve children on the verge of puberty, particularly girls.

There are a great many other precedents for the kind of events that happened in Abbott Road, Winton, in 1981. They have occurred throughout recorded history all over the world. Some incidents, including Enfield and the Durweston case reported above, have been extremely well documented by credible witnesses such as professional investigators, writers, policemen and public officials. Each case is unique but striking similarities to other cases are often apparent. The sound of knocking, rapping and footsteps, the movement of heavy furniture, objects flying through the air and damage and destruction of various kinds are all typical symptoms of poltergeist activity; the activities often give the impression that they have been directed by an intelligence. Written messages have been known to appear, as at Durweston, and in some cases the intelligence even seems to

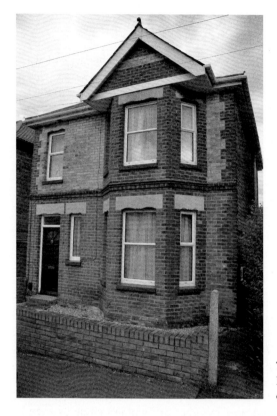

The Burden family's home at 37 Abbot Road, Bournemouth, has changed little since the dramatic poltergeist events in 1981.

have a sense of humour. The first serious investigator of poltergeists, Allan Kardec, wrote in the nineteenth century of a case in which such knocking turned out to indicate that a friendly spirit was trying to deliver a message. Once the message had been delivered, the rapping stopped. Also typical is the involvement of a young child, often at the age of puberty. The Winton case also involved children, though not apparently of pubescent age. In the Abbott Road household, it was eight-year-old Bradley who attracted most attention. After her visit, Miriam Jeffreys said, 'I feel this thing is in Bradley. But he is not being naughty. It is a thing from the devil – a force of light.'

In the *Bournemouth Times* on 22 August 1981, David Haith wrote:

Charles is convinced the boy is somehow the innocent focus for the poltergeist energy. Throughout the haunting he has rarely shown any emotion. He watches the proceedings quietly with a smile. Witnesses who have seen him closing his eyes, pressing his ears and shaking his head have wondered if the force is working through him. He also admits to having an invisible playmate.

The story continued:

Alone with Bradley in a wrecked room after one of the poltergeist outbreaks, I found the boy in exuberant mood. He constantly darted about picking up toys and broken ornaments and motioning to throw them towards me, all with a mischievous grin. Suddenly, while my back was turned, a tin crashed down from a sideboard, spilling biscuits over the floor. Was it Bradley... or the ghost?

Almost certainly the boy had toppled the tin but several witnesses have told me they have seen objects move when Bradley was not close by. Could he, like Uri Geller, possess psychic powers to influence matter? There were similar poltergeist outbreaks at the home of [the] now famous psychic Matthew Manning. He later went on to bend spoons, Geller-style, and now has channelled his abilities into new fields. In experiments he has managed to influence cancer cells in test tubes and recently drew huge crowds as a healer and acclaimed worker of miracles. So perhaps Bradley – being tagged the ghost boy by the national media – may after all have a happy future.

Noreen Penfold – who was particularly close to Bradley and looked after him during the two weeks immediately following the Abbott Road happenings – remained convinced that the boy was the unwitting victim of a troubled spirit. When I interviewed her in 1989 for *Ten Dorset Mysteries*, she recalled that he had himself had a troubled life before joining the family as a foster child.

'We had him from the age of two and when he came he couldn't talk properly,' she said. 'He used to sit in the corner and make noises like a dog. He was a lovely, lovely kid who just wanted love but was incapable of showing love himself. If he was put to bed at night, he wouldn't sleep but would wander around the house. His eyes were black and when he looked at you he had piercing eyes like in the film *Damien*. He only had to look at a bonfire and it would flare up. He was always talking about his friend, Ian, saying that Ian had told him to do so and so, and then laughing.'

Mrs Penfold also recalled that the second séance identified the 'troubled spirit' not as the neighbour who had hanged himself but as a member of Debbie's circle of friends, who had died at an early age.

> The spirit was a drug addict who had died and come back through Bradley. He had shown himself to Bradley as a boy but when all this happened he showed himself as a man. It wasn't very nice at the second séance, apparently. There was a lot of bad language and a lot of cursing because he was a troubled spirit. They found out that his name was Ian and he had known Debbie and had come through Bradley, who was an open channel, an easy channel, because he was retarded. They found out about Ian's addiction and how he died. All he wanted to do was be at peace. Eventually they brought his nan through and they kept saying, 'Do you see the light? Do you see the light?' He said he did and reached out and held his nan's hand. Once through, the voice changed and he said it was beautiful and he was at peace.

Mrs Penfold's interpretation of the Abbott Road events is consistent with one of the leading theories about the nature of poltergeists, namely that ghosts, or spirits of the dead, are able to manifest themselves by somehow absorbing and using energy from their victims. A second theory is that some people, particularly boys and girls at the age of puberty, are able to extrude a force or energy which is capable of intelligent action.

The second séance does seem to have been effective, for the Burden family were never troubled by poltergeist activity after that time nor, as far as is known, have any later occupants of 37 Abbott Road. Despite the apparently positive outcome, however, the havoc had taken its toll on the family, who never were completely reunited. After a few days away from the house, Charles and Kathy felt they could no longer cope with Bradley and asked that he be taken back into care. They never saw him again. Eight years later, Charles Burden told me:

> My wife just couldn't cope any more. Her nerves were smashed and we couldn't look after him. We couldn't blame Bradley for what happened but I believe the spirit picked on him because he was backward. A university professor who came to investigate told me it mostly comes with backward children. It wasn't something Bradley could help. But things only happened when he was around and stopped happening after he had gone. I don't know where he is now. I believe he went to a family in another county and was going to be adopted.

Charles, Kathy and Debbie returned to 37 Abbott Road after a week but they also resolved to leave as soon as possible. The house was placed on the market and three months later was sold to a single man who was convinced the poltergeist would not return. The Burdens moved to Wallisdown and later to Parkstone. Debbie moved to the London area, married and started a family.

THE LEGLESS MILKMAID

The old Pamphill milking parlour, which once supplied milk and dairy products to the Bankes family of Kingston Lacy House, near Wimborne, is today a thriving farm shop with adjoining restaurant. But tales told by staff and customers suggest that one of the old milkmaids may not have moved on. Former employees tell how they would go to get out the horse feed only to find that the job had already been done for them, or how, if they left a tap on, some unseen figure would turn it off.

Stephen Tucker, now a Wimborne ambulance man and retained fireman, personally saw the ghostly milkmaid several times when he worked at Pamphill in about 1997.

> It was usually at dusk and it looked as if she didn't have any legs – she just seemed to glide or float along outside the farm shop and restaurant. Several others saw the outline of a milkmaid, including customers. When a customer asked for horse feed, we had to get it from a barn at the back, which was kept locked. A couple of times, I went to get the feed and found that what the customer wanted was already in the trolley.

According to Stephen's mother, Deirdre Tucker, one visiting customer – unaware of the ghost stories – announced that she could see the ghost of a milkmaid standing in the restaurant. 'The customer was obviously sensitive to these things and even said that the ghost had given her name,' says Deirdre. 'Stephen and others actually went looking for the name in Kingston Lacy churchyard nearby but they didn't find anything.'

Even more intriguingly, the customer commented that she could not see the milkmaid's feet or lower legs. 'Investigations later established that the present building has a higher floor than its predecessor, suggesting that the milkmaid's feet were at the level of the old floor,' Deidre added.

CHAPTER SIX

MODERN MYSTERIES

A VICTORIAN CLAIRVOYANT

Robert Young, who was born at Sturminster Newton in 1811 and died there in 1908, is best known as a writer of humorous verse in the Dorset dialect and his memories of his native town in the nineteenth century. But his recollections, published in full for the first time in 2008, also include what can only be described as a perfect description of remote viewing or astral travel. Young did not use those terms, of course, but it's clear that this is the kind of phenomenon he was referring to when he describes what he witnessed during a visit to his son in Wales.

In his own account, Young tells how his son introduced him to an old Welshman called Davis, who had never set foot outside his own native community. Young said:

> I spent several evenings in his company and was surprised at what I heard from his lips after he had passed into what appeared a sound sleep. The way in which that sleep was produced was as follows: soft music was played on the harmonium, music of an imposing nature. The hand of my son made passes over him a few times – and then he was asked if he was ready to answer any questions put to him. The first question was to visit my home [in Sturminster Newton] and give a description of it. To my surprise, he gave a PERFECT description of the house and its surroundings. And of persons he described there, of that I knew nothing – but on my returning home I found [it] was true.

To test the Welshman's abilities, Young took a letter from his pocket book and asked him if he could tell whether its writer was a man or a woman. He placed the letter on his forehead and said it was a man who wrote it, which was correct. Asked if he could locate the writer of the letter, the Welshman was silent for five minutes. Then, moving his hand slowly, he said, 'I am in a strange country. I have found him.'

Asked to describe the man, he went on, 'He is sitting in a room with a young lady – I believe his daughter. His dress is peculiar and he wears a velvet cap. He has a wonderful head. The work of his brain would kill a great number of men.'

Young was left in no doubt that the man described was his old friend and fellow Dorset dialect poet William Barnes. 'From the perfect description he gave,' he says, 'I knew it was Mr Barnes, and the letter I gave him was one I had received from the above.'

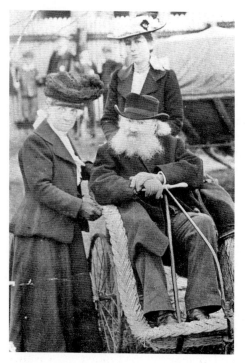

Dorset would probably have seemed like a 'strange country' to a Welshman who had never left his native community. But there was more. 'Each evening he underwent the same treatment and gave an account of what was passing at home, which on enquiry when I arrived home was TRUE TO THE LETTER,' says Young. 'I could fill several pages of this little book and give the names and places he described with perfect accuracy. I told my friends what I have described but the general public would not believe it if I told them. The time is not yet come. But it is coming. Another pen than mine may some day give a full account.'

Alas, no other pen appears to have given a full account, but Young would no doubt be happy to know that the old Welshman's talents are by no means unique. There is a vast and growing number of such instances on record; I personally know several people with the ability to astral travel at will and at least three who have consciously developed this talent in order to view remotely.

The Dorset dialect poet Robert Young saw clairvoyance, or remote viewing, first-hand.

THE TEN OF DIAMONDS

Although only in his fifties, Percy Benjamin Newport was in 'indifferent health' when he came to live with his son-in-law and daughter, Mr and Mrs Herbert Faulkener, in the village of Leigh, near Sherborne, in the 1920s. In fact his health was so poor that he had to spend his mornings in bed. One morning in January 1927, as she was doing her housework, Mrs Faulkener heard her father cry out. She hurried upstairs to find him sitting up in bed and gazing intently at something.

'Look, look!' he cried. 'That nurse! She has a black pot with hot, steaming stuff in it. And a card, the ten of diamonds. Take it away from her – take it away. She is threatening me. She'll empty the boiling stuff over my head if you don't take the card away.'

Mrs Faulkener could see no nurse and no playing card. She tried to calm her father but he was insistent and kept asking her to 'take the card away from her and that will save me'. Eventually he recovered sufficiently to dress and come downstairs but he still insisted that the ten of diamonds needed to be taken out and burnt.

The following day Percy Newport returned to his home town of Frome, Somerset, where he had worked as a butcher for many years. He was due to have an operation at the Victoria Hospital where, exactly ten days later, he died. The funeral procession began on foot from Percy Newport's brother's house in Frome with the coffin placed on a bier on the garden path. As the chief mourners took their places next to the bier, Mr Faulkener looked at the ground and, to his amazement, saw a playing card – the ten of diamonds. He nudged the dead man's brother, who was next to him but knew nothing of the strange events at Leigh a couple of weeks earlier. He too saw the card lying on the path. Neither man wanted to disturb the funeral procession so they left the card where it was – but when they returned shortly after it had vanished, even though no one else had entered the garden in the meantime.

Soon after, Percy Newport's brother visited the home of his niece and her husband at Leigh. A game of cards was suggested and a new pack was opened. Upon the seal being broken and the cards checked, one was found to be missing – the ten of diamonds. It proved to be the final twist in the strangest of mysteries – a mystery that has never been solved. According to Percy Newport's family, he had always been fond of playing cards but had no interest or belief in psychic or paranormal phenomena.

FAIRIES IN THE GARDEN

Sir Arthur Conan Doyle is best known as the creator of Sherlock Holmes but he began his adult life as a doctor and in later life developed a fanatical interest in the supernatural. Unfortunately his reputation was seriously damaged after he famously championed photographs purporting to show diminutive fairies cavorting with people. The pictures of the 'Cottingley fairies' turned out to be fakes produced by two schoolgirls with a parent's camera. However, in his book *The Coming of the Fairies* (1922), Doyle describes another fairy episode witnessed in a Poole garden by his friends Vincent N. Turvey, author of *The Beginnings of Seership* and 'one of the most gifted clairvoyants in England', and Mr Lonsdale, of Bournemouth, also a 'well-known sensitive'. Happily, there were no photographs to discredit the story – or, or course, to confirm it.

According to Conan Doyle, Lonsdale told him:

I was sitting in his [Turvey's] company in his garden at Branksome Park. We sat in a hut, which had an open front looking on to the lawn. We had been perfectly quiet for some time, neither talking nor moving, as was often our habit. Suddenly I was conscious of a movement on the edge of the lawn, which on that side went up to a grove of pine trees. Looking closely, I saw several little figures dressed in brown peering through the bushes. They remained quiet for a few minutes and then disappeared. In a few seconds a dozen or more small people, about two feet in height, in bright clothes and with radiant faces, ran on to the lawn, dancing hither and thither. I glanced at Turvey to see if he saw anything, and whispered, 'Do you see them?' He nodded. These fairies played about, gradually approaching the hut. One little fellow, bolder than the others, came to a croquet hoop close to the hut and, using the hoop as a horizontal bar, turned round and round it, much to our amusement. Some of the others watched him, while others danced about, not in any set dance, but seemingly moving in sheer joy. This continued for four or five minutes, when suddenly, evidently in response to some signal or warning from those dressed in brown, who had remained at the edge of the lawn, they all ran into the wood. Just then a maid appeared coming from the house with tea. Never was tea so unwelcome, as evidently its appearance was the cause of the disappearance of our little visitors.

Lonsdale said he had seen fairies several times in the New Forest but never so clearly. Conan Doyle commented on two common features with other sightings of fairies: it occurred 'in the heat of a summer day' and featured 'the division of the fairies into two different sorts'.

'Knowing Mr Lonsdale, as I do, to be a responsible, well-balanced and honourable man, I find such evidence as this very hard to put to one side,' Conan Doyle wrote. Referring to his earlier discussion on the subject, he added, 'Here at least the sunstroke hypothesis is negatived, since both men sat in the shade of the hut and corroborated the observation of the other. On the other hand, each of the men ... was supernormal in psychic development, so that it might well happen that the maid, for example, would not have seen the fairies, even if she had arrived earlier upon the scene.'

Fairies, as Conan Doyle discovered, are a topic calculated to push the boundaries of credibility even more than ghosts, UFOs and most other less-than-earthly phenomena. Perhaps that's why fewer people are prepared to own up to such experiences, or even admit them to themselves. There are exceptions, however, and as recently as June 2009 I interviewed an elderly couple about the 'great number of fairies, elves and dwarves' who regularly appeared near their former home in Verwood in the 1970s.

Marie Williams has made good use of her clairvoyant abilities during her eighty years and used to lecture on spiritual matters for the Churches Fellowship for Psychical and Spiritual Studies. Her husband, Douglas, is a retired schoolteacher. In 1969, when Verwood was still a scattered heathland village with a fraction of the population it has now, the couple moved into a bungalow called Heathlands in Ringwood Road, almost opposite what is now the Ebblake Industrial Estate. It had nine acres of land, much of which was covered in heather. Within the heather were the remains of a circular earthwork and inside this was a 'perfect ring or circle' formed by seven or eight mature silver birch trees. Marie and Douglas also found what they call a 'seer-stone' inside the circle. They came to believe that the site had seen a 'tremendous amount of spiritual activity' in the past.

The couple's two Airedale terriers seemed to agree. One of them, which Marie describes as an 'old soul', would never enter the circle; the other dog, in contrast, regularly went 'straight in and ran in circles until she fell down'.

'Quite a number of times I saw groups of "men" from the outer worlds joining up together in that circle,' said Marie. 'You could see the glow around them. It was really wonderful.'

What Marie and Douglas (and almost certainly Sir Arthur Conan Doyle and his friends) are talking about is nature spirits. This may be an alien concept even to many readers whose belief systems embrace some of the other topics covered in this book. However, there are many who believe in 'invisible' nature spirits, working behind the scenes to assist in the propagation of flowers, vegetables and other plants. The Findhorn Community in Scotland, most famous for its magnificent vegetables grown in poor soil, is the modern world's best example of human beings consciously co-operating with nature spirits.

Douglas Williams said:

Marie actually saw the 'ship' coming and going between our plane and their plane. On occasions I was there and she would say, 'Look! Look! There it is!' But I couldn't see it. I could only see an aura or mist. Marie was seeing clairvoyantly but I could feel the tremendous power from it. We seem to have been very blessed in that we have only encountered good from this. There is never any feeling other than a pure sort of love and understanding and a desire to be of assistance.

By the time Douglas and Marie left the property in the late 1970s, the once scattered village of Verwood had become the fastest-growing town in Europe. Their home was about to be engulfed by a sea of modern bungalows.

'The nature spirits knew that we were leaving and that the land was going to be built on and there was nothing more for them,' says Marie. Her husband adds, 'On the day we left, they left like a huge cloud from the big circle in that hollow. Not because we were leaving but because they knew it was the end of an era because the land was going to be built on.'

THE PORTLAND BLADE

It was about 10 p.m. on a fairly clear night in the summer of 1973 or 1974 when Margaret Lewis and her then boyfriend, Patrick, witnessed a strange phenomenon at Portland. They were standing next to the Trinity House Monument looking towards the lighthouse at Portland Bill when a thick fog suddenly descended. A fog on the Dorset coast was not in itself unusual but what followed certainly was.

'The fog completely obscured the lighthouse and, as it did so, a silver metallic blade appeared,' says Margaret, from Stalbridge. 'It was right in front of us – standing vertically, stationary and silent. The blade was 2ft to 3ft wide and the part we could see was about 6ft tall – but some of it was not visible because of the fog. It was so close – about 3ft in front of us – that we could have reached out and touched it.'

The blade remained visible and stationary for about thirty seconds before rising rapidly and disappearing silently into the fog, which then cleared as quickly as it had arrived, bringing the lighthouse back into view.

The couple never reported the event, which has remained a mystery to Margaret ever since. Many years later, however, she and her husband, Barry Thomas, bought a book on UFOs which included a chapter on the Moigns Down craft seen in 1967 by Angus Brooks and reported in the final section of this book. As that also involved a blade-like object only a few miles across Weymouth Bay, Margaret and Barry have often wondered if the two events were connected.

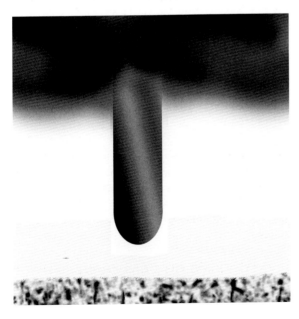

An artist's impression of the Portland Blade, based on Margaret Lewis' own drawing.

The Portland incident was not Margaret's first encounter with the unexplained nor was it to be her last. She and her twin sister, Jane, were aged about ten in 1961 and living with their parents in a chalet bungalow in Thornhill Road, Stalbridge. Ghostly appearances are more commonly associated with older properties but their home had been built only a year earlier.

About 6 o'clock one evening, when it was still fairly light, Jane left the sitting-room to go to the bathroom but immediately rushed back in saying there was a little old lady in old-fashioned costume in the hallway. She was afraid to re-enter the hallway so Margaret agreed to accompany her – and she too saw the figure.

She looked at me and Jane and I asked her what her name was. She didn't speak. She just looked at us and half-smiled. I felt she could see us. She was an elderly lady and about 5ft tall – not much taller than we were then. You could see it was an apparition but she was solid – you couldn't see through her. She was wearing a black skirt and an apron and old-fashioned glasses. Her clothes were definitely from a past era – maybe fifteenth or sixteenth century. Her hair was in a bun and she looked about eighty. After I spoke, she half-smiled, made her way towards the kitchen door and disappeared into the kitchen. Throughout this our Alsatian dog remained asleep in a basket under the stars.

The girls never saw the old lady again and their parents remained fairly sceptical. About twenty years later, however, long after the twins had left home, their father had cause to revise his opinion. At about 3 a.m. one night, Patrick Lewis emerged from the bathroom into the hallway and saw the old lady moving towards the front door. She then appeared to open the door with the handle, walk through and close the door behind her. Thinking it might be his wife, Joan, he called out to her but received no response. He then went back to the bedroom and found Joan still in bed – and never doubted his daughters again.

'The land where the bungalow stands was previously a meadow but we did wonder if it was on the site of a footpath into Stalbridge, which was perhaps used by the old lady when she was alive,' says Margaret.

While many people go through their whole lives without experiencing the paranormal first-hand, many others seem destined to have a range of experiences, perhaps because of their natural psychic abilities. Margaret Thomas appears to be one of these. In the early 1980s, when she and Barry were running a dry-cleaning business at Clock House, Sturminster Newton, she had a near-death experience. Margaret, wearing high-heeled shoes, was taking down the Christmas decorations when she twisted her ankle badly. Barry caught her but she passed out with the pain and swallowed her tongue.

Barry said I went rigid and my colour changed from scarlet to black. He put me on my side and tried to resuscitate me and my colour came back. What I remember is waking up in a dark space and something telling me to turn around. I was on a stage and could see quite a bright light. There were people in the distance and something told me it was my relatives. I could see them at different heights. They were solid and wearing ordinary clothes that I could remember them by. I seemed to be quick-marching towards them but I couldn't see my own legs. I said to the people, "Oh, dear. I think I'm in heaven. I can't leave Barry to run the shop on his own." With that I came back into my body. It was a marvellous experience and I felt privileged that my creator allowed me to come back alive. I always feel that when my time comes I shall go knowing there is life after death.

A few years after this Margaret and Barry shared another UFO-type experience while working together on the 2.30 p.m. to 10.30 p.m. shift for a food company at Chard, Somerset. Barry says:

> The sighting occurred at 5.45p.m. on November 2, 1990. We were walking across the factory yard when our attention was drawn to a large triangular object in the sky above the factory car park to our left. The object had pure white lights around its underside perimeter and was gliding slowly and silently at a very low altitude from east to west. The object appeared to be grey against the clear dark sky and seemed to be fairly flat. The altitude seemed to be about twice that of an average two-storey house. Using the car park as a point of reference, the estimated length from its apex to its base was 200 to 250 feet. We viewed the object for several seconds as it travelled slowly over trees and a housing estate, eventually disappearing from view.

Barry adds:

> We have no idea what the object was but it was definitely not a conventional aircraft. Nor was it an airship, a balloon, the planet Venus or lights reflected from low clouds. There was no sound. To the best of our knowledge, we were the only witnesses, as no reports appeared in the local papers or on local radio or television. We find it difficult to understand why no one saw such a large object at such a low altitude.

Further research by Margaret and Barry revealed that during 1989-90, large triangular objects were seen in the skies over Belgium. 'These objects were reported to have three white lights on their underside and not the same lighting pattern as the object we both witnessed. The Belgian objects were said to be travelling at a "gliding speed" and some witnesses reported them accelerating rapidly and disappearing at "tremendous speeds without a sound".'

DORSET DOPPELGANGERS

Part of thirty-year-old Adrian Brown's job as a supervisor for a security company in 1991 involved driving a van around south-east Dorset checking on various sites. He usually stuck to a strict timetable but was running twenty minutes late on one occasion as he approached a roundabout at Holton Heath, between Wareham and Lytchett Minster. As he drove around the roundabout, he looked across and could not believe what he saw. Driving around a different part of the roundabout, lit up by the lights of a lorry, was a white van identical to the one Mr Brown himself was driving. It even had the same distinctive black lettering on the side. When he looked to see who was driving, the person turned his head towards him – and he recognised himself, even down to the moustache he wore at that time.

Adrian Brown was no publicity-seeker and it was not until a reporter from *The Advertiser* heard a rumour three or four years later and tracked him down that his story became public. 'I can't describe that uneasy feeling in that split-second when we looked at each other,' he told the reporter, David Haith. 'It was an emotion which started in the pit of my stomach which I have never experienced before.'

Mr Brown completed his journey and his work but admitted that he felt 'stunned' and 'frightened' when he reached his home in Heathwood Road, Winton, Bournemouth. Next day, he inquired about the whereabouts of the only other van owned by his company and matching the description. What he already knew was confirmed – it was off the road after breaking down.

Thinking about the incident later, it occurred to Mr Brown that it took place at the very time he would normally have been driving around the roundabout from the opposite direction had he not been twenty minutes late. The incident worried him for some time afterwards as he considered such explanations as the theory of parallel universes. 'What if I'm not really here and the guy driving the other van is the real Adrian?' he asked.

Adrian's experience sounds like a classic case of the doppelganger – albeit with the addition of a distinctive van. There are a great many such incidents on record and in modern occult thinking the phenomenon is explained as a temporary detachment of the 'subtle body' from the physical body with which it normally coincides. Mr Brown's experience is reminiscent of an event described by Johann Wolfgang von Goethe in his autobiography. The German poet was walking along a road in Alsace after visiting his girlfriend when he saw his own apparition approaching, dressed in a grey and gold suit. Eight years later he was on his way to visit the same girl when he suddenly realised that he was wearing the same grey and gold suit at the very same spot.

Both Goethe and Adrian Brown were seeing their own doppelgangers but a more common phenomenon is the observation of someone else's double by a third party. A few weeks after his story on Mr Brown appeared, David Haith was contacted by a family living near Broadstone who had an experience of this kind to describe. The story was never published at the request of the family, who said they had been 'traumatised' by the events which unfolded in December 1994. Fifteen years later they have requested anonymity so for this first published account I have changed their names to John and Patricia Perkins and their daughters, Melanie, fourteen, Rebecca, thirteen, and twelve-year-old Lucy.

The episode occurred two weeks before Christmas as John, Patricia, Lucy and Melanie arrived home after a shopping trip. Patricia recalls:

> We were surprised to see our other daughter, Rebecca, standing on the doorstep in the cold with her school friend, Heather. Both looked worried and shocked to see us. Looking at Lucy and Melanie, Rebecca said something like, 'How can you be here with Mum and Dad? We've just seen you upstairs in the house'. They told us they had been so frightened by something that had happened in the house that they were standing outside until we came home. Rebecca said they were too scared to go back in alone.

Rebecca herself describes how she and Heather opened the front door and immediately heard the voices of Melanie and Lucy coming from an upstairs bedroom. They climbed the stairs and, as they neared the bedroom's closed door, the voices sounded louder but oddly different. They sounded 'mechanical and robotic – almost Dalek-like'. 'They were talking about Christmas and we got the impression the two of them were wrapping presents.'

Rebecca and Heather were so unnerved that they ran down the stairs and out of the house. After a short time outside, they decided they were being silly and plucked up the courage to go back in. Cautiously, they opened the door and immediately saw a figure peering down at them from the top of the stairs. 'It was Lucy but she was saying nothing and staring so intently that it gave me the creeps,' says Rebecca. 'It was so scary that we ran outside again.'

When the 'real' Lucy and Melanie stepped out of the family car with their parents, Rebecca and Heather were 'freaked out', as they put it. 'I really don't know what to make of this except to say the girls inside were somehow the doubles of the girls outside,' Patricia adds.

CHAPTER SEVEN

CLOSE ENCOUNTERS

THE FLYING CROSS OF MOIGNS DOWN

As UFO witnesses go, it would be hard to find many better qualified or more credible than J. W. B. 'Angus' Brooks. He had spent most of his working life in aviation, serving as an RAF intelligence officer during the Second World War and as a Comet flight administration officer with BOAC subsequently. The 'family man in his fifties' was also described as a 'prime example of a man of common sense, who would not dream of inventing a sighting for the sake of personal publicity'. He was clearly rational with no history of hallucinations and no particular interest in UFO reports. That is, until 26 October 1967.

At 11.25 a.m. that morning, Mr Brooks and his two dogs, a Dalmatian and an Alsatian, were taking their daily walk on Moigns Down, between the village of Owermoigne, where he lived, and the Dorset coast at Ringstead Bay. The sky was clear, apart from a small amount of low cloud, but there was a force-8 wind. In order to shelter from the wind, Mr Brooks lay on his back in a hollow. He had hardly had time to position himself with his hands behind his head when he saw what he at first thought was an aircraft's vapour trail over Portland. However, he soon realised that it was not a vapour trail because instead of lengthening or spreading before dispersing, it descended at an incredible speed to about 200 or 300ft, at which point it decelerated abruptly, levelled off and hovered above the ground about 400yds from where he lay. There it remained for twenty-two minutes.

Mr Brooks described the object as having a drum-like chamber at its centre from which protruded four girder-like 'fuselages'. He estimated that the drum was about 25ft in diameter and 12ft thick and that each 'fuselage' was 75ft long, 7ft high and 8ft wide. These dimensions gave it a total diameter, from tip to tip, which Mr Brooks estimated at 175ft.

As the object swooped in over the coast towards him, one of the fuselages was pointing ahead while the other three trailed behind 'like the feathers of a bird's tail'. Then, as it hung in the air, the two outer rear fuselages fanned out to 90° angles, with the other two forming a flying cross centred around the drum-like chamber. Mr Brooks noted that the craft had no windows and appeared to be made of a translucent material which changed colour to match the sky. Each fuselage had a nose cone and beneath each were dark shadows which seemed to indicate grooves. It remained silent throughout.

Mr Brooks was in no doubt that he was viewing an alien craft. When UFO writer Robert Chapman visited the lonely Moigns Down with him some months later, Mr Brooks told him:

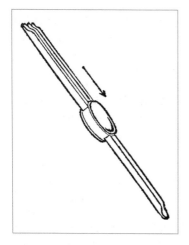

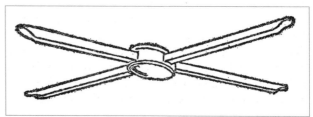

Left: The 'arrival' position of the Moigns Down UFO, with its fuselages folded.

Above: The Moigns Down craft with fuselages in hovering position. Both sketches from Robert Chapman's book *UFO: Flying Saucers Over Britain?*

To begin with I was apprehensive, wondering if I had been spotted. It even crossed my mind that I might be captured and I planned, if there seemed any danger of that, to leave my walking stick in the ground as a clue to where I had been. But after a bit I felt easier, even content, and it has since occurred to me that the green anorak I was wearing may have camouflaged me.

Mr Brooks's twelve-year-old Alsatian, Tana, was certainly not content. While his other dog had run off in search of rabbits, Tana became very agitated, ignoring her master's orders to sit and repeatedly pawing him as if urging him to leave the area. After hovering for twenty-two minutes, the craft reverted to its original formation, with one fuselage at the front (though not the same one) and the other three trailing behind. Then it shot away at increasing speed and disappeared high in the sky over Winfrith.

After initially deciding not to tell anyone about the experience for fear of ridicule, Mr Brooks eventually told his wife, the local vicar (who was an ex-police officer) and Weymouth police, and also consulted both the Atomic Energy Research Establishment at Winfrith and a USAAF communications unit at Ringstead Bay to ask if anything unusual had been observed. It hadn't. Nor did any other witnesses come forward after the sighting was reported on radio and television – although that may not be too surprising, as Moigns Down is rather remote.

The Ministry of Defence took Mr Brooks so seriously that they despatched a team of three well-qualified professionals to investigate – a scientist and a psychologist from the RAF and a writer attached to the Ministry of Defence secretariat. Their conclusions were no less bizarre than the incident they were investigating. In a 1,000-word report, they suggested that what Mr Brooks saw was not an alien craft at all but a 'vitreous floater' – dead matter in the fluid of his eyeball – and that this had somehow been dramatised because he had been dreaming after falling asleep or entering a sleep-like state. The supporting evidence for this theory included the fact that Mr Brooks had once suffered an eye injury, since repaired by a corneal transplant, and that after walking across rough terrain in a gale, he might have been tired enough to fall asleep on the downs; they also implied that Mr Brooks may have been influenced by the large amount of publicity given to other UFO sightings during the previous month.

Six months after the sighting, Mr Brooks sent a point-by-point response to the investigators. He pointed out that there had in fact been corroborative reports in the area involving night sightings of star- and dart-shaped objects, both of which sounded similar to 'his' craft. He included evidence from his eye specialist to dismiss the 'floater' theory, adding, 'As my eyes were not stationary during the twenty-two-minute observation, the chances of the exact similar shaped MV (muscae volitanties) being present in both eyes at the exact same time can be discounted.' On the suggestion that he fell asleep, he commented, '... as for sleeping on route – please! The fact that the gale was howling and my Alsatian was painfully clawing me to leave the spot was hardly conducive to "dropping off".' Mr Brooks concluded, 'Your conclusions have not given me cause to alter my opinions of the Moigne Downs [sic] UFO.'

An observation that may be relevant in this case is that many of the most intriguing UFO incidents have occurred near key military sites – including the most famous in America (Roswell, 1947) and Britain (Rendlesham Forest, Suffolk, 1980). Angus Brooks' sighting occurred within a triangle formed by the Winfrith Atomic Energy Research Station, Portland Underwater Defence Station and the USAAF Communications Unit at Ringstead Bay. While many people dismiss such sightings as merely the products of people's imaginations or delusion, there are other plausible theories. One is that people have spotted secret craft or weaponry developed by the earthly superpowers. Another is that the sightings involve alien civilizations, which are observing military equipment or even protecting us from our own folly by neutralising atomic weaponry.

One of the other sightings referred to by Angus Brooks in his response to the investigation had occurred only thirty-six hours before his, on the night of 24 October 1967 when two policemen in the neighbouring county of Devon followed a vast illuminated flying cross for twelve miles along the edge of Dartmoor. Similar sightings were reported in other parts of the country on the same night. This could be interpreted as supporting evidence of Mr Brooks' sighting, but the Ministry of Defence team chose an opposite interpretation.

Eleven days after the Moigns Down incident, between 1 and 2 a.m. on 6 November 1967 (some sources say 11.30 p.m. on 5 November, although there is no suggestion that fireworks were involved), there was an equally intriguing event less than 40 miles to the east. On the old A338 road between the villages of Avon and Sopley, at a spot which was then 4 miles into Hampshire but is now just a few yards on the Hampshire side of its border with Dorset, a lorry and a Jaguar car approaching from opposite directions simultaneously ground to a halt. While the Jaguar's engine cut out altogether, the motionless lorry's diesel engine (which did not depend on an electrical ignition system) kept running. Both drivers and the Jaguar's woman passenger then watched in amazement as an egg-shaped object moved across the road in front of them at a height of 25ft and then gradually accelerated and disappeared. After it had passed, the Jaguar's engine sprang back to life.

The lorry driver, Carl Farlow, estimated the length of the craft at 80ft (it was overhanging both verges at the same time) and described it as magenta-coloured with a white base. It gave off a smell like that of a drill boring through wood and sounded like a refrigerator. Mr Farlow called the police from a nearby call box and begged the Jaguar driver, a veterinary surgeon, to stay and back up his claim but he refused, as he had been drinking. Police found that the road surface had melted and next day, when Mr Farlow returned for his truck, he found a bulldozer levelling the road, a painter working on the phone box and other people examining the area with instruments. When he drove along the road a week later, he found that a 70yd stretch had been resurfaced.

What on earth was going on in Dorset and the adjoining counties in the late autumn of 1967? It's a question that has never been satisfactorily answered.

UFO SCOOP FOR CARL

On 12 February 1973, Bournemouth newspaper reporter Carl Whiteley wrote the story he had waited years to write. 'For forty-five breathtaking minutes early yesterday, I watched a mysterious disc-shaped object travelling across the clear, moonlit sky,' he wrote in that day's *Evening Echo*. 'It was like a huge luminous wheel and it moved silently, slowly on its end in a straight line from west to south. As it came closer, it appeared to be rotating.'

Carl was one of the *Evening Echo*'s most experienced journalists with a reputation for sound, accurate reporting and not a hint of sensationalism. He was also one of my most respected *Evening Echo* colleagues from the day I joined the paper in 1975 until his premature death while on duty as an auxiliary coastguard in 1981.

It was also during coastguard duty that he saw his UFO. Visibility was exceptionally good in the early hours of 11 February 1973, as Carl and his coastguard colleague Mike Parker, a Mudeford fisherman, kept watch on the Channel from the lookout hut at Hengistbury Head. They were armed with binoculars powerful enough to pick out cars at Swanage, 12 miles across Poole Bay. There being no maritime dramas to occupy his attention, Carl pointed the binoculars towards the westerly sky to view the stars.

'Through the mass of twinkling lights emerged a moving light high over the Purbecks,' he said. 'At first it gave the impression of a luminous tube. But as it moved southwards its circular shape became apparent. It was not an aircraft and it could not have been a cloud or a weather balloon for it later returned westward against the wind, banking at an angle as it disappeared.'

Carl likened the UFO to 'a phantom gliding through the night sky'. But he added that it was not visible to the naked eye and must have been 'at a vast height and, being so high, one can assume it was of great size'.

'Over the years I have reported other people's sightings but this was my own observation,' Carl continued. 'And Mike Parker was my witness. He, too, saw the mystery object. Some twenty years ago Mike and his brother, Charles, saw a cigar-shaped object in the sky while night-fishing at Mudeford.'

Carl's report added, 'Is there another world? Could it be that people from that world are watching us? My sighting does not answer those questions. But it convinces me that UFOs exist...'

ETHEL'S CLOSE ENCOUNTER

Late one evening in September 1977, sixty-two-year-old Mrs Ethel Field was removing washing from the clothes-line in the back garden of her home in Sea View Road, Parkstone, Poole, when a humming sound prompted her to look up at the sky. It was a clear night and she immediately saw, approaching from the south-west, what she described as a round object with a dome on top. The dome appeared to have two windows, which extended to about two-thirds of the height of the object and one-quarter of its circumference. There could also have been 'something on the dome', she added, but events moved so quickly she could not be certain of this. There were other things of which she was certain, however.

UFO investigator Leslie Harris wrote in a report for *Flying Saucer Review* and the UFO Information Network (UFOIN):

The object was emitting light of a brilliant intensity, the object itself glowing with a greyish colour, whilst from around the perimeter of the disc, light of a much more brilliant bluey-yellow colour beamed downward, giving the overall impression of an umbrella shape. This light did not illuminate anything on the ground, and Mrs Field did not notice how far down it extended. Beneath the object, Mrs Field thought she saw a 'patterned' effect but was unsure on this point and unable to elaborate.

Mrs Field found it difficult to estimate the size of the object but eventually concluded that it must have been the width of her garden (22ft). The altitude presented even more of a challenge but she agreed that it could not have been particularly high, as she was able to see two humanoid occupants, one standing at each window. The cabin appeared to be normally lit.

When the craft reached a point immediately above the far end of the garden, it hovered for a moment and Mrs Field put up her hands, palms outwards, to shade her eyes from the brilliant light. At this point, she felt a slight sensation of heat on her hands. For one or two seconds, the ground under her feet trembled and she wondered if there was about to be an earthquake. She was surprised that no one came running out of their houses.

Mrs Field described the occupants of the craft as being of normal proportions. They were wearing silver suits with headgear of the same colour, which covered all but the face and came to a point at the forehead but appeared to be separate from the suit. She believed there was a collar but she did not recall seeing any buttons or fasteners. Mrs Field said the faces of the occupants had 'slender features' and she had the impression that both were male. Their arms were of normal appearance but their hands matched the colour of the suit, suggesting that gloves were being worn, although Mrs Field was uncertain about that. The being on the right from Mrs Field's viewpoint was looking down as if operating controls just below the window. The other one looked straight at Mrs Field, moved over slightly and made a pointing gesture with his right hand which she took to mean that he was intending to land.

Mr Harris, a former editor of *Scan* magazine, estimated that the episode had lasted no more than twenty or thirty seconds before Mrs Field fled to the house. At the back door, she paused and looked back just in time to see the object heading at speed to the north-west.

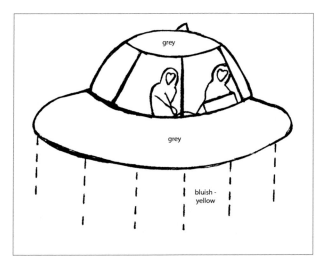

Dave Till's sketch of the UFO and occupants seen by Ethel Field from her Parkstone garden in 1977.

The startled housewife then rushed indoors, where her husband, Maurice, sixty-eight, and daughter, Teresa, twenty-four, were watching television and reported no interference with the reception. When Mrs Field related her tale, her family just laughed at her. Teresa persuaded her not to phone the local paper on the grounds that people were likely to ridicule her. However, some weeks after the sighting, Mrs Field responded to a public appeal for people who had had UFO experiences to attend the opening night of *Close Encounters of the Third Kind* as guests of the Gaumont Cinema in Bournemouth. Leslie Harris was given the task of 'sorting the wheat from the chaff', as he put it, and was sufficiently intrigued by Mrs Field's story that he paid her two visits, on 22 March and 6 April 1978. This was six or seven months after the event. Mr Harris reported:

When I first arrived at Mrs Field's home, she apologised for being unable to shake hands with me, as she had a skin infection. At the end of our interview she told me that this trouble had begun the week following her sighting with a spot in the palm of her left hand. This had spread and worsened until both hands were raw and very painful. Her doctor diagnosed dermatitis and treated her for this. I examined her hands and found them to be very dry, with the skin peeling. At no time did Mrs Field claim that this condition had been caused by her UFO experience. She mentioned it only as an afterthought and said she was 'keeping an open mind' about the cause. However, bearing in mind, said Mr Harris, that (a) during her sighting Mrs Field shielded her eyes from the intense light of the object WITH PALMS FACING OUTWARDS; (b) she felt a slight sensation of HEAT ON HER HANDS whilst doing this; (c) the trouble developed the week following her sighting and she had never before suffered from a condition of this kind; and (d) my dictionary definition of dermatitis is 'inflammation of the skin by localised irritation, eg external burning by the sun, X-rays, etc', I felt it worth presenting this as tentative evidence of a possible UFO-related physical after-effect.

Mrs Field's story subsequently found its way into not only the *Bournemouth Times* and *Poole and Dorset Herald* but also most of the national dailies. This was not something Mrs Field had sought and even Mr Harris was appalled at the 'inaccuracies, exaggerations and downright fabrications' contained in the reports. He said:

One report said that 'a saucer swooped on her' – a totally inaccurate and misleading statement. Reports of 'burns' were gross exaggerations of the actual condition of her hands. But the worst example of press distortion was the widely publicised statement that 'coastguards saw it too'. This was just not true. It arose when a reporter from BBC Radio Solent visited Mrs Field and happened to mention that his father, an auxiliary coastguard, once saw a UFO. That such a chance remark could be so grossly distorted is, to me, incredible.

Mr Harris added:

I have no reason to believe that the story told by Mrs Field is other than the complete truth. She wanted no publicity, her family laughed at her and she made no play at all of the condition of her hands, a point she could easily have used as direct evidence in her favour. She co-operated willingly with me but now wishes to see no more reporters or investigators. If her story seems a little lacking in precise detail, it must be borne in mind that she was suddenly confronted with a phenomenon totally outside her experience, that she was alarmed, and only observed it for a brief period of time before running to the house. My view is that here we have a very normal sixty-two-year-old housewife, of limited vocabulary, attempting to describe an event which was real to her. And that is surely what matters.

THE FLYING BURGER

At about 4 p.m. on 13 November 1980, six young boys were playing football on parkland known as Baiter Point on the edge of Poole Harbour when one of them noticed something unusual above Parkstone Bay. Anthony Rayment shouted to his friends, who saw what they described as an object about twice the size of a helicopter and stationary at about 300ft and an angle of 45°. They likened its shape to that of 'a hamburger with bumps' and bisected horizontally by a black band. They watched the object for about three minutes, at which point it began to rise before flying slowly away on a diagonal course. The boys, all aged nine and pupils at nearby South Road Combined School, were still in a state of high excitement – and all 'talking at once' – when Anthony's mother arrived to meet him. This was at the very conclusion of the sighting and by the time she became aware of the cause of the excitement, the object had disappeared from view.

The episode was investigated by Leslie Harris and Ron Lucas, with Leslie's report appearing in *Flying Saucer Review*. They questioned five of the boys – Anthony Rayment, Richard Gillson, Lee Perkins, Matthew Anderson and Vincent Jones – but were unable to talk to the sixth, Abdul Shahid, due to the 'reserved and suspicious nature' of his guardians. Abdul was, however, interviewed at his school by the *Poole and Dorset Herald*, telling them he would 'not like to see a UFO again'.

While the accounts given by the other five had much in common, there were also some discrepancies, although this may be seen as adding to rather than detracting from the credibility of their story. You need only to sit through a few court cases or inquests to know that even adult witnesses frequently contradict each other when describing the same incident.

All five boys agreed that the object was 'hamburger-shaped' or oval and that it had 'bumps' which they found difficult to describe. Anthony said it had 'bumps on top' and a 'jagged bottom' while Lee said there were 'rows of bumps on top and bottom'. Matthew, Richard and Lee all described a black line bisecting the object across the centre but Anthony described it as a 'black surround to base'.

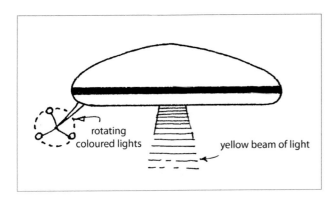

The burger-shaped UFO seen by six boys from Baiter Point, Poole, in 1980. Re-drawn from a sketch originally published in *Flying Saucer Review*.

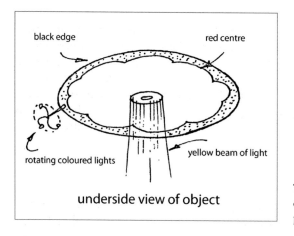

The underside of the burger-shaped object. Re-drawn from a sketch originally published in *Flying Saucer Review*.

Lee and Richard respectively gave the colour of the UFO as 'whitey-grey' and 'silver-grey' but Matthew said it had 'red and green squares', Anthony saw 'red and green checks' while Vincent thought it was 'blue, yellow and red'. Richard believed it had a propeller protruding diagonally downwards from the left side with red, yellow and blue lights that were rotating at 2rps. Lee also reported red, yellow and blue lights but believed they were static and that the colours changed. But both he and Matthew were convinced that the propeller protruded horizontally from the object's right side. Matthew also described a second protrusion pointing downwards with a constant white light at its end. Vincent had not noticed any kind of propeller.

Anthony, who was closest to the object as well as the first to see it, claimed to have had a clear view of the underside, describing it as a 'red poppy shape' surrounded by a black border and with a yellow light which shone from a protrusion in the middle of the base. Richard also mentioned the poppy shape which, he said, grew dimmer before the object disappeared.

Only Lee Perkins could remember hearing any sound, describing a 'low, humming' noise. Matthew thought that Anthony had spoken at the time of 'a sound like he'd never heard before' but Anthony had no recollection of this.

Lee Perkins seemed to be the most psychologically affected by the experience, describing how his initial excitement and shock turned to fear after he got home. He subsequently dreamt about a UFO landing, taking two boys on board and the firing of guns. He woke up with a scream and began waking up screaming roughly every other night for some time afterwards. Vincent Jones, on the other hand, seemed 'somewhat disinterested' in the whole business, although he co-operated with the interview.

The investigators concluded that the boys were unlikely to have made up their story, and Leslie Harris wrote at the time:

If they did, they were far more cunning that one could reasonably expect of nine year olds. Why make conflicting statements regarding certain features of the object? We interviewed each boy separately and all appeared most sensible, honest and anxious to recall the details of their experience as accurately as possible for our benefit. Our opinion is that no deliberate hoax was perpetrated but that the boys witnessed a phenomenon totally outside their normal experience and therefore had difficulty in relating the details without inconsistencies as confirmation rather than denial of the presence of a true unknown.

Almost thirty years later, Matthew Anderson and Lee Perkins, who both live in Poole, are still unable to explain the experience. 'It's a long time ago and we were very young but we definitely saw something and I don't know what it is to this day,' says Matthew, of Canford Heath. Tragically, Anthony Rayment died of a brain tumour within two years of the incident. As he was the first to see the UFO and the closest to it, some of the other parents wondered if the object had somehow contributed to his death – through some dangerous emission, for example. There is, however, no evidence of this.

THE STAPEHILL TRIANGLE

Angie Costello (née Till) believes she was aged about thirteen when she had her close encounter, which would put the date at about 1983. She was a pupil at Queen Elizabeth's School, Wimborne, but was at home in The Vineries on Colehill's southern slopes when the incident occurred. 'It was a nice cool day and I was walking through our bungalow with an armful of books when all of a sudden this huge thing went past the window,' she recalls. 'It was cigar-shaped, silver in colour and had windows, although I don't remember seeing anything through the windows. I would describe the shape as something like a Zeppelin. It was really close – just a couple of arms' length away from me – and so large that it filled the whole of the two big windows on that side of the bungalow. It may sound strange but it seemed to be heading right through our garden hedge. It was a bit of a shock. I called the rest of the family to come and look but by the time they got there it had gone.'

It would tempting to dismiss Angie's story as the imaginings of a young girl were it not for the events which unfolded a short distance away on the same day. 'That evening the girl down the road, Charlotte Newman, had something land in her field. The grass was burnt in four places, suggesting that something with four legs had landed there,' says Angie. What she was not aware of was that her experience was at least the fourth apparent 'close encounter' within a very small area in the space of twenty years.

Less than a mile to the south-east of the Vineries is 5 Stapehill Crescent, which in 1963 was the home of sixteen-year-old Angela Powell, her thirteen-year-old brother, Alan, and their parents, Ron and Joyce. The family had moved to Stapehill from the Bristol area a few months earlier and Angela had begun work as a trainee receptionist at the King's Head Hotel in Wimborne. In adult life, as Dr Angela Thompson Smith, she has become a practitioner and teacher of remote viewing in the USA and the author of several books but as a girl she had a number of experiences of a kind which typically affect people who are psychically gifted. In one of her books, *Remote Perceptions: Out-of-Body Experiences, Remote Viewing and Other Normal Abilities*, she describes how, from the age of eight, she would spontaneously astral travel before going to sleep at night. 'I recognised that these experiences were very different to sleeping dreams' she says. 'I was awake when they happened. I would sit up on a roof and look around or travel down the country lanes of suburban Bristol. These out-of-body experiences were spontaneous and random, and occurred without my direction. Later I was able to bring them under some control.'

Angela's experience at Stapehill in 1963, however, was of the passive rather than the active kind. In another book, *Diary of an Abduction: A Scientist Probes the Enigma of her Alien Contact*, she writes:

Our house had a large, long garden, mostly meadow, and at the bottom of the garden was a stand of old elm trees, a tiny brook, and beyond that more rough meadows. Alan and I had separate bedrooms. One night in the spring of 1963, at about 10 p.m., our rooms were lit up with an intensely bright light. My brother looked out of his bedroom window and said that a flying saucer had landed in the meadow beyond the brook. I was very frightened and hid under the bedclothes but I could still see the light. Alan continued looking and said that people had come out of the flying saucer and were moving around. Later, the light went out as suddenly as it came on, and it was totally dark. The next morning neither our parents nor anybody else in the neighbourhood mentioned seeing the light. Following that night, I suffered from terrible nightmares in which I would be squeezing through small spaces before arriving at a long, grey room. There, at the end of the room, was a box-like table and I would experience the most incredible terror.

More than forty-five years later Angela remains convinced that the experience was real and that her brother did not make up or exaggerate what he saw after she dived under the sheets. 'Alan and I shared everything and, although he was a fearless little devil, he was usually honest with me. I still believe that what he saw was the real thing. I remember being very afraid and asking Alan, "Are they still there?" He said, "Yes." Then, all of a sudden, the light went out as suddenly as it had come on. We talked about the event for years.'

In February or March 1979, sixteen years after Angela Thompson Smith's experience, postman Alan Waters was riding his 50cc motorcycle from his in-laws' home in Ferndown to his workbase at the Wimborne sorting office when he had a close encounter of the first kind. 'It was certainly winter because there was ice and slush on the road and I was having to take great care,' he recalls. 'I started work at 4 a.m. so the time would have been about 3.45 a.m. and it was pitch black.'

Alan's journey took him through Hampreston crossroads and along a bendy stretch of Ham Lane – the section that has been called Old Ham Lane since the opening of the Wimborne by-pass in the early 1980s. This is only about 200 to 300yds from Stapehill Crescent. In his wing mirror Alan saw the reflection of a light approaching at speed on his right hand side. 'It was going quite fast and I remember thinking, "Stupid idiot",' says Alan. 'I lost it in my mirror but then suddenly it came right up beside me on the left, lighting up the hedgerow and me and the whole area. I didn't see any objects or anything – just this intense, extraordinary light that seemed to be on me. I thought that perhaps someone had gone through the hedge. I was feeling very strange and very confused. When I got to work, I told a couple of colleagues about it.'

That evening, Alan read in the *Evening Echo* that a couple on their way home from a party at about 4 a.m. had reported seeing a mysterious bright light in the sky. 'From their description, it was in the same area as I was. They said it appeared and disappeared as quick as lightning. Thirty years later, I really have no explanation for it. I just know it was something that wasn't normal. It was too bright and coming too fast. It seemed to stay with me for seconds. Then suddenly it had gone and it was completely black again.'

From 1970 to 1981, former Colehill parish councillor Elsie Sanderson and her family lived at 19 Olivers Way, Colehill, just 400yds east of The Vineries and two-thirds of a mile north-west of Stapehill Crescent. Like The Vineries, Olivers Way is on the southern slopes of Colehill overlooking the valley that includes the other two locations. 'I can remember it as clearly as if it was yesterday, although I don't know when it happened,' said Elsie in 2008. 'My bedroom overlooked pasture land with just a single oak tree and the disused railway line all the way down to what was then the A31 road. One night I woke up to find my bedroom filled with light. It was a brilliant light, more blue than white. I don't know what it was but I have never forgotten it.'

Before the light disappeared, Elsie had time to get out of bed, go to the toilet and return to the room. 'I had just got back into the bedroom when the light went out. Next morning I told my husband but he said I must have imagined it. There was nothing to see the following day but I'm sure I didn't imagine it.'

The occurrence of unexplained happenings in geographical clusters is a recognised phenomenon among UFO investigators. The most famous location is the Bermuda Triangle, although so-called evidence of UFO links with the disappearance of ships and aircraft in the region has been largely discredited since the 1970s. According to *The Mammoth Encyclopedia of Extraterrestrial Encounters*, 'the British Isles has one of the highest incidence rates for UFO sightings in the world, but reports are not scattered randomly around the country'. The most notable hotspots have been Warminster in Wiltshire in the 1960s, Bonnybridge in Scotland more recently and 'UFO Alley', an area of east Lancashire and west Yorkshire, which has provided 10% of all UK sightings and some of the most intriguing. Although The Vineries incident in Dorset was reported in a local paper at the time, the other three in the Stapehill-Colehill cluster have come to light only in the last few years.

SUMMONED BY AN ALIEN

It was early on a May morning in 1986 when a Wareham housewife woke at dawn with what she described as 'the feeling that I was being summoned'. She prefers not to be identified for fear of ridicule, but when I interviewed her in 2008 she told me:

My husband remained asleep and the dog was snoozing at the bottom of the stairs. I was like a zombie. I felt I was being told to go downstairs and through the lounge and to open the curtains. I looked across and at the far end of my neighbour's garden, I saw a putty grey-coloured being but it wasn't human. It had a traditional ET-type appearance. The face was oval, the eyes slanted and the mouth closed. I don't think there was any hair and I don't remember there being a nose. There was something on the upper arms rather like rolled up shirt-sleeves. It was staring straight at me as if it was taking all the knowledge that I had. I found myself thinking I didn't have much knowledge to take! Eventually I came to and got goosebumps up my back. I was frightened and went back to bed. I never told my husband, as he wouldn't have believed me, and I only told my daughter about it many years later.

STAIRWAY TO ANOTHER DIMENSION

Like many ancient sites, Knowlton, a few yards from the Wimborne to Cranborne road, has had a magnetic pull on people for millennia. The centrepiece is a derelict fourteenth-century church, its roof and fittings long departed and even its walls incomplete. Surrounding this ruin are the circular banks of a Neolithic henge and beyond that is a scattering of Bronze Age round barrows. In the field to the east a large round mound of Neolithic origin lines up with the henge, the church and the equinox sunrise.

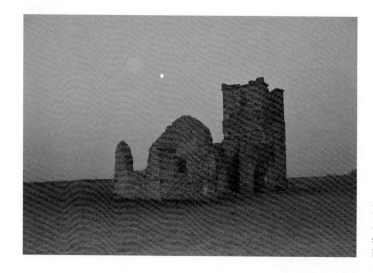

Knowlton church and the Moon at the spring equinox sunrise in 2003. Photograph by Peter Knight.

There would once have been standing stones here but only a handful remain. A dowser recently discovered one, buried under the topsoil. Another appears to have been used as a cornerstone by the church's builders. On another corner, a stone buttress has been worn down at waist height by the hands of generations who have sought to experience the three energy lines that are said to converge here. Some detect the energy as a rocking motion; others feel the flow as a spiral. 'It's either where the stone used to be and where the energy is still rising or perhaps it's where the three lines meet,' says Peter Knight, a writer and public speaker on ancient sites. 'If you have energy lines across a field and you stand a stone on it, it fixes it down. It's a bit like an acupuncture needle going into your skin. It will amplify the energy as well as well as storing it like a rechargeable battery.'

Many people have reported unusual experiences at Knowlton but few will have had an encounter quite as strange as that which happened to Geoffrey Lindley, of Branksome Wood Road, Bournemouth. When I first read his own written account, I could not decide whether it was intended to be read as fact or fiction. We arranged to meet at Knowlton, where Geoffrey told me:

> It's subjective but to me it was a real experience with a real craft and real beings. And I hadn't been drinking! As soon as I got home, I was telling colleagues all about it. I'm sure they were ready to call in men in white coats. There seems to be a current explosion of spirituality, not necessarily relating to a specific religion, and I would hazard a guess that my experience relates to that. People are thinking about the states of consciousness and how they think and how they act. I think it's important to relate that experience and also how to interpret it.

The experience which Geoffrey describes as 'mind-blowing' began around 3 p.m. on 'an atmospheric day when the sun hung low in the sky and the shadows were lengthening'. He had walked only 15yds towards the monument when 'suddenly the surrounding countryside reverberated with the glorious, exultant sound of Led Zeppelin performing their transcendent "hymn" Stairway to Heaven'. The music lasted only a few seconds before silence returned and Geoffrey continued to the ruined church, where he noticed a man and a woman standing by one of the inside walls. However, this was no ordinary man or woman.

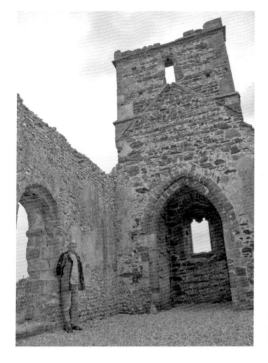

Geoffrey Lindley at the exact spot where the golden-haired man and woman were standing in the ruins of Knowlton church.

He says:

They both had golden hair, looked about 30 years of age and radiated tranquillity. I acknowledged their presence with a smile and mentioned that I was visiting the church for the first time. They told me they had been visiting the area for 2,500 years. When I asked how this was possible, they said they were members of the Illuminati and had conquered the ageing process.

'How have you done that?' Geoffrey asked.
'We have expanded our consciousness and have become completely detached from the world of emotion.'
'This can't be much fun.'
'You should seriously consider the fact that a permanent state of quiet ecstasy is possible if one is capable of finding the joy that is to be found in experiencing the awareness of one's existence.'

Geoffrey's account continues:

Following this advice, I was told to look upwards and, gazing into the sky, I saw a brightly shining saucer-shaped object that I estimated was at least 500 metres in diameter. I gazed open-mouthed as it moved towards the horizon at incredible speed and within a couple of seconds it had vanished from view. When I looked back into the church, the two individuals had disappeared and I have not seen them since.

Many readers will no doubt find Geoffrey's story hard to believe but after meeting him I was convinced that at the very least the experience was real enough to him. Beyond that, who are the rest of us to judge? I know many others who claim to have had mind-opening experiences that are often stranger than science fiction and seem to be designed specifically for them. This was certainly the case with Geoffrey Lindley.

'My experience has caused me to think deeply about the nature of reality and I am convinced that, beyond the limits of our senses, there are other dimensions of existence,' he says. 'I believe I entered another dimension during my visit to Knowlton church.'

A MESSAGE FROM SPACE?

At 5.12 p.m. on 26 November 1977, hundreds of thousands of television viewers in Dorset and other southern counties were startled by an interruption to their nightly news programme on the ITV regional station Southern Television. Although the pictures from the studio continued as normal, for five-and-a-half minutes the sound was overridden by another broadcast which appeared to be a message from outer space. The message, delivered in a severely distorted voice but a calm and deliberate manner, began:

> This is the voice of Gramaha, the representative of the Ashtar [some sources say Asta] Galactic Command, speaking to you. For many years now you have seen us as lights in the skies. We speak to you now in peace and wisdom, as we have done to your brothers and sisters all over this, your planet Earth. We come to warn you of the destiny of your race and your world so that you may communicate to your fellow beings the course you must take to avoid the disasters which threaten your world and the beings on our worlds around you. This is in order that you may share in the great awakening, as the planet passes into the New Age of Aquarius. The New Age can be a time of great peace and evolution for your race, but only if your rulers are made aware of the evil forces that can overshadow their judgements.
>
> Be still now and listen, for your chance may not come again. For many years your scientists, governments and generals have not heeded our warnings; they have continued to experiment with the evil forces of what you call nuclear energy. Atomic bombs can destroy the earth and the beings of your sister worlds in a moment. The wastes from atomic power systems will poison your planet for many thousands of your years to come. We, who have followed the path of evolution for far longer than you, have long since realised this – that atomic energy is always directed against life. It has no peaceful application. Its use, and research into its use, must be ceased at once or you all risk destruction. All weapons of evil must be removed.
>
> The time of conflict is now past and the race of which you are a part may proceed to the highest planes of evolution if you show yourselves worthy to do this. You have but a short time to learn to live together in peace and goodwill. Small groups all over the planet are learning this, and exist to pass on the light of the dawning New Age to you all. You are free to accept or reject their teachings, but only those who learn to live in peace will pass to the higher realms of spiritual evolution.
>
> Hear now the voice of Gramaha, the representative of the Ashtar Galactic Command speaking to you. Be aware also that there are **many false prophets** and guides operating on your world. They will suck your energy from you – the energy you all know as money – and will put it to evil ends giving you worthless dross in return. Your inner divine self will protect you from this. You must learn to be sensitive to the voice within, that can tell you what is truth, and what is confusion, chaos and untruth. Learn to listen to the voice of truth which is within you, and you will lead yourselves on to the path of evolution.

This is our message to you, our dear friends. We have watched you growing for many years as you too have watched our lights in your skies. You know that we are here, and that there are more beings on and around your earth than your scientists admit. We are deeply concerned about you and your path towards the light, and will do all we can to help you. Have no fears, seek only to know yourselves and live in harmony with the ways of your planet Earth.

We of the Ashtar Galactic Command thank you for your attention. We are now leaving the planes of your existence. May you be blessed by the supreme love and truth of the Cosmos.

The studios of Southern Television were inundated with calls from worried viewers and the broadcaster issued a statement blaming the incident on 'students'. 'We have a fair idea of how it happened but obviously we cannot release the details, as this would encourage another hoax,' they said. They claimed that only the transmitter at Hannington, near Newbury, had been affected. The hoaxer was thought to have used his own transmitter to fade the incoming signal and replace it with his own.

An investigation was launched in an attempt to catch the culprits but more than three decades later those responsible remain unidentified and the broadcaster's explanation remains controversial. 'The amount of expensive equipment needed to overpower a powerful television transmitter takes the incident out of the realm of a college prank,' says the Church of Ufology website. Janet and Colin Bord, authors of *Modern Mysteries of Britain*, agree: 'Very sophisticated equipment would be needed to achieve what the "hoaxers" did achieve, and it would also have had to be very high powered to put their signal into the relay station at Hannington. The authorities were uncertain as to how it had been done, despite their apparent confidence that it was a hoax.' Some sources suggest that the message went out from no less than five transmitters, not only Hannington. The original audio-tape can even be downloaded from the Crowded Skies website (http://www.crowdedskies.com/download_files.htm)

Whether or not it was a hoax, the 'voice' certainly spoke a great deal of sense and echoed the underlying views of many in the modern world. The essence of the message and even some of the phraseology will be familiar to anyone acquainted with the vast amount of New Age literature that has been published in recent years, and especially the vast number of messages that have been channelled through mediums around the planet. The Ashtar Galactic Command also feature prominently as the alleged source of some channelled messages dating back to the 1940s.

For me personally, the broadcast was reminiscent of the Nine, who delivered hundreds of hours of channelled messages spanning several decades through the American medium Phyllis Schlemmer. In one communication, the Nine declared that there were extra-terrestrials 'now working on the technology of interfering with television transmissions and projecting their own material on to television screens, as this was considered a good way of demonstrating their existence to a large number of people at once'.

Interestingly, this statement and other Nine communications first appeared in print in Stuart Holroyd's book *Prelude to the Landing on Planet Earth*, published in 1977. Could it be that the overriding of the Southern TV broadcast in November of that year was an example of such activity – perhaps even a test run? Or was it the contents in Holroyd's book that put the idea into the mind of a clever hoaxer with electronic know-how, more than a passing acquaintance of New Age thinking and the ability to imitate channelled communications? It may indeed have been a hoax. But what if it wasn't…?

BIBLIOGRAPHY

BOOKS

Beaminster Museum, *The Book of Beaminster* (2007)
Bennet-Stanford, J, *Monmouth, The Rebel: His Flight* (1937)
Bord, Jane & Colin, *Modern Mysteries of Britain* (1987)
Brookesmith, Peter, *UFO, The Complete Sightings Catalogue* (1995)
Chapman, Robert, *UFO, Flying Saucers Over Britain?* (1969)
Dorset Year Book 1949-50
Ellis, Chris, & Andy Owens, *Haunted Dorset* (2004)
Evans, Hilary, *Seeing Ghosts, Experiences of the Paranormal* (2002)
Forde Abbey and Gardens, *850 Years of History* (guide)
Guttridge, Roger, *Ten Dorset Mysteries* (1989)
Harwood, Julie, *Haunted Poole* (2007)
Holroyd, Stuart, *Prelude to the Landing on Planet Earth* (1977, reprinted 1979 as *Briefing for the Landing on Planet Earth*)
Hutchins, John (and continuators), *History of Dorset* (1774)
Ingram, John H., *The Haunted Homes and Family Traditions of Great Britain* (1905)
Joire, Paul, *Psychical and Supernormal Phenomena, Their Observation and Experimentation* (1916)
Legg, Rodney, *Mysterious Dorset* (1987)
Legg, Rodney, Mary Collier & Tom Perrott, *Ghosts of Dorset, Devon and Somerset* (1974)
Ludlam, Harry, *The Restless Ghost of Ladye Place and Other Hauntings* (1967)
Playfair, Guy Lyon, *The Haunted Pub Guide* (1985)
Price, Robert, *UFOs Over Hampshire and the Isle of Wight*
Sheppard, Dick, *The Unexplained* (c.1984)
Udal, John Symonds, *Dorsetshire Folk-lore* (1922)
Underwood, Peter, *Ghosts of Dorset* (1988)
Young, Robert (ed Alan Chedzoy), *Early Years, Recollections of Life in Sturminster Newton in the Early 19th Century* (2008)

PERIODICALS

Bridport News, Evening/Daily Echo (Bournemouth), Bournemouth Times/Poole and Dorset Herald, Bournemouth and Poole Advertiser series, Flying Saucer Review, Pulman's Weekly News, Gentleman's Magazine.